Forged In Ink

Forged In Ink

a collection of poetry and prose from the soul

AVANT AVANT-GARDE

300 SOUTH MEDIA GROUP

NEW YORK

ISBN-13— 978-1-957596-08-2

First Printing September 2022

Cover & Interior Design by Indie Author Solutions
Published by 300 South Media Group

To the inspirations,
The hope keepers,
The grab the bull by the horn while crying fighters,
My Phoenix risers

> *—I see your forge and thank you for blowing the*
> *winds to fan my own*

Special Dedication—

To my #'s, plus the glam squad—the reasons that I do all that life
requires

> *—for you all, I would harness the sun and ride it*
> > *—I love you, so.*

TABLE OF CONTENTS

DEDICATION   v

ACKNOWLEDGMENTS   xiii

FOREWORD   xv

INTRODUCTION   xvii

DYSLEXIC   1

MIRRORS   3

ASTUTE   5

BATTLE SCARS   5

SNOW WHITE   6

REFLECTIONS   6

AROMA   9

COUNTERPARTS   10

PAINTBRUSH   11

LOUNGING   13

DOUBLE VISION   15

STRUCK   16

ANTICIPATION   17

PASSION & PERSPECTIVE   18

ASTROLOGY   18

DISNEY   19

GUST   21

DOUSED   21

REASONS   22

ETCH N SKETCH   23

SUCCUMB   24

BRANDED   24

GLANCES   26
LEGACY   28
TANGO   29
REST   30
TOTAL ECLIPSE   30
A WHIRLED WIN   31
ERECTED   32
ARTISTRY   33
COLORED   33
BED REST   34
TWISTED   34
GEOGRAPHY   35
INTERTWINED   36
REMBRANDT   37
FALLEN ANGEL   38
JOUSTING   38
KEYS   39
XENA   40
WIZARD   40
STRIPPED   41
DIVE   42
HEAVENLIES   42
GROUPIE   43
MONSTER INK   43
ECHOED   44
PROMINENCE   45
SUBDUED   46
BALM   47
GENERATIONS   48
FROST BITE   49
LUCK   49

PLEDGE	50
DELIVERY	51
SECONDHAND HEARTS	53
INFUSED	54
ORBIT	55
WHITE	56
ALWAYS	56
TRACED	57
INHALES	58
SHEET MUSIC	58
TAINTED	59
REVITALIZED	59
PIECES	60
COVET	61
DAMPENED	62
FORNICATIONS	64
SAFE	65
ASHES	67
DESERT	72
MISTRESS	73
ASPHYXIA	73
RIVALRY	74
INCISIONS	74
DESICCATED	75
TARNISHED	75
CEMETERY	76
HEMORRHAGE	77
DRESSED	77
PROGENY	78
TEMPEST	80

ENIGMA   81
PARADOXES   82
SULLY   83
WARNINGS   84
A MOTHERLESS CHILD   91
BLUDGEON   92
OBEDIENCE   92
HOCUS POCUS   93
CALL   94
GRETEL   95
MOTHER GOOSE   95
COSTUMES   96
THERAPY   97
FRAGILE   98
INFERNO   98
SHARPSHOOTER   99
ADULTHOOD   100
TOUCHED   101
REPUTE   101
VAGRANT   102
TONE DEAF   103
TRAVESTY   103
GAMBLE   105
SPLATTER   105
FURY   107

NAKED   109

BARE   110
STRUCK   110
CREATION   112

INKED 112

TANGIBLE 113

ACHE 114

DITTY 115

VORACIOUS 116

DESOLATIONS 116

RENDERED 117

SEAMSTRESS 117

BATHED 118

PERMANENT 119

FINGERPAINT 120

NOVICE 121

ASPHYXIA 121

FOREPLAY 122

SEQUENCE 123

CHANNEL 123

MANTRA 124

SMEAR 125

WHISKEY 126

FIRST 127

SOILED 127

NEAT 128

MOONLIGHTING 128

SCRIBBLES 129

PARCHED 129

DAYDREAMS 130

SALUTED 130

SIGNAL 131

OXYGEN 132

ADDICTION 132

AFTERBURN 133

PORTRAIT   134
PEELED   134
INTOXICATED   135
SIPS   136
BECKON   136
CORNUCOPIAS   137
DRENCHED   137
OWN   138
GLISTEN   138
RUB   139
ACROSTIC   139
CHURCH   140
SIGNALS   141

SKIN   143

SCHOOL DAZE   152

FINAL WORD   183

ABOUT THE AUTHOR   183

ACKNOWLEDGMENTS

RLKH, what can I say that you don't already know—thank you goes without saying and so does love you, ALWAYS!!

My dad, who is the epitome of what love looks like in flesh—love you

To my Peanut, the one who has loved me and stood by me all his life—no matter what or how! You are my little, big brother. I love you with all my soul and will search the earth over to find additional if that isn't enough. You know why I thank you. Let this be the door closing at last. Bubbie, Bubba, Brina— I love you to pieces and always will, big sissy out!

My Sunflower, if you only knew what you mean and will always mean to this soul of mine—I love you, heffa!

K.K., Mirs, Alpine & Bossman—you came in, turned my soul upside down, and I found out my ink could defy gravity—thank you with all my heart and every bit of my soul

My dream team—Abbs, LeeLee, Mags, Cuddles, CB, Sweetpea, Whip, Mocha, & Hardhead, y'all made this possible every day, all day—you are irreplaceable, love you

My Unwounded, Butterfly — you are a graceful butterfly sighting. You are a heart teaching lungs how to breathe—I love you, so very much. Thank you for everything!

In my life, there are Tweety birds and Music boxes, with Lyrics of gifts, known as Le Stars. Wildfires that dance near, Coffee-mates, with Butterfly wings, opening Closet Doors. As Dragonflies hoover over Dandelions with Pen staining Paper at hand, Poetry Elegance can be seen & Every Emotion, as I bask in heavenly Resa Cups. So enchanting, to find Nerds, that Wright, in Writes of

Stiletto glory, strumming Strings of Flames. Where Lace Terrorizes in beauty and kick, as Monsters in ink, leave prints across the soul howling. There are so many more, who create moments like none other—thank you, you have no idea what your life signifies in my own —if I ever nicknamed you, then this is for you too lol...

Do you realize how precious you are to my fellow writers and endless smiles in the community?

You are the lighthouse amongst the waves of those searching for written paths through the crash—never dim

  —A. Avant-garde

FOREWORD

When I met Avant Avant-Garde, the first thing I noticed about her was how giving she was and how generous she was with her light. If you know her, you know she shines it everywhere and shares it with everyone who needs it. I love that about her.

She's a rare gem and I tell her that often.

She knows what it is to be broken, and she has carried more than most could ever imagine.

In her own words, she once told me that she just wants people to be seen and to feel worthy—things she was never told or shown.

She acts from her heart and soul. She doesn't know how to be any other way. It's in her being.

I'm quite certain her first language is poetry. If you've ever interacted with Avant Avant-Garde, I'm sure you will agree.

Her writing is breathtaking, soulful, passionate, and raw—evoking such powerful emotions. She turns pain into poetry. Avant Avant-Garde writes on life— reflections, pain and hurt experienced from relationships and abuse, as well as sensuality, and self-acceptance.

Her words will touch your heart and hug your soul. Her words aren't just poetry, they are a journey.

—Kristin Kory (Author of Hungry For Ghosts)

INTRODUCTION

When I sat down to ink, all I could think of were the moments in my life that had dried with stains, still ran wet with smudges, and bottles of thoughts that I had yet to spill onto blank pages. I was curious as to how my eclectic ways of taking sensory and lines, would blend together to paint a canvas worthy of you—the reader. I didn't want to just write poems or prose. I wanted more than just micro cliches of thoughts on lines. I wanted a story within each story of what just being real while trying to figure out what overcoming the hands of life looked like—Sometimes clear, other times messy, many times bloody, but always unfolding. As you read, give your soul space to breathe, if you have been in those moments, I'm proud of you for the past tense. If you are still there, you can do it, leave footprints across the back of pain and run away with peace.

These are just moments in life, that have been seen, lived, survived, etched, haunted, and became fingerprints upon the hands of process as one might try and fail at life...

Avant Avant-garde

DYSLEXIC

Tired of unlearning,
To relearn,
To be not learned...

"Proverbial student of life," you say,
The things that come, the things that played.

The moments true, the moments false,
The moments for foreign, domestic life wars— of loss.

The things that grasp first,
Then set us free,
The moments we live in victory...

The times when we are broken,
The times when we rise,
The living between lines of truth and stains of lies.

Here I stand, this student in life,
Taking test after test, of heartache and plights.

The mind, a worn-out pencil.
This soul, paper—cuts
Living as third-degree burns, from eraser marks...

The Alma Mata— lyric-less,
Understanding academics, but never graduating
Failing at everything, while
studying hope and plagiarizing.
I'm tired of learning backward...

FORGED ◆ IN ◆ INK

MIRRORS

The inventor of the mirror poisoned the human heart…

Fernando Pessoa

I sat at the table, dropping tears of courage into coffee like it had been my favorite creamer all along. How had life opened the doors to nothing, so widely— I wondered out loud. Always the perfect hostess to rise— greet the fight, breathe in your fear, and beat the breaks off resolve— these had been my breakfast companions through the most horrific of blows life had to offer and yet, I am now a violent mute, sitting across the table from a total stranger—Myself. My soul had become like a quadriplegic— "will chair" bound to stagnation. More creamer to the coffee, a pour without permission; yet here the sip comes, the bittersweetness of learning all over again...

ASTUTE

Tired of unlearning,
To relearn,
To be... not learned
While walking around—a Wikipedia of others

BATTLE SCARS

Weary of fighting,
Identity growling
Low crawling into breathing—Tired...

I didn't sign up for this,
I was drafted
Like sunlight, coerced into sharing warmth to the wetness that seeks
dryness
Railroaded, like the moonlight, is ransacked by star-crossed lovers
needing one last peek—Tired...

Obligations kept calling me to war and my honor had battle fatigue.

SNOW WHITE

Mirror, Mirror of my soul
*Show me why this **Reckoning** holds*
My hair in flames just like my life
My eyes are dark, a reflection of this knight
My lips, wine-stained, that's the shade I call blood
I'd gladly take the apple if
It frees me from this tug—

REFLECTIONS

Eyes are never silent
The soul, it never whispers
Touch is rarely mute
That is why I taste you in every pause I exhale

You hear about it all the time, those who have "loved, lost, rebirthed —self..." and yet, here I am, staring once again at a table setting with no one but this shadow of my lifeless, soul— I am tired. My identity has "shaken life syndrome" and I am tattered and shattered; dehydrated tears and a drowning spirit stuck in the reservoirs of depletion lie in silence. I tried speaking, but I feel like I speak a foreign language to my destiny as the G.P.S. of my life refuses to change course. No matter how often I attempt to scream, my hopelessness can only whisper crescendos under the water of obligations. I sip just a little longer, hoping that the moment of awaking will subside; I know it won't and I catch a glimpse of my reflection in the cup—coffee stains of war paint still dripping down my lips, yet I sip...

I changed my clothes like he changed his moods. Time to be and do as I was groomed. As I pulled the clothes off the hangers, a picture of us fell that had been under some boxes. Better days. Back when he first looked at me as if the sky had whispered to him that I was the inspiration for sunsets. Back when he took time to listen to my thoughts spoken and unspoken, like I was his favorite program, and he was going through the DVR to not miss an episode. Back when I could just think his name and my soul would perfume and slip into something comfortable... back... the land before time. I picked up the picture and flipped it face down— shoving it back under the boxes.

AROMA

You're on my heart like a tattoo
Dripping inked prints down the
Walls of my soul's veins
Like a pulse is a photo album reflecting what is complete
I thumb through the pages of your etch
        —leaving initials within my smile's skin
And just like that,
 I taste your essence upon the lips of my yes
        *—**Exhales** leaving photographic memories of your scent...*

COUNTERPARTS

Souls that have found mates
forged not found
carved through tears and subsided fears
poured into the mold of compromise
chiseled into the image of unity
reflections of love fought
lessons acquired and humility taught
not the high of convenience
or just stumbled across
they are the hands that see our pieces
and choose to sit with our jigsaw puzzles

> **patiently**

Heart full of grief,
Slipping on the oil of choices
The past now bandaged together with turmoil
Lessons of who we were stripped of sedations
As love buckles under the pain
And open chest wounds hemorrhage into complacent smiles

PAINTBRUSH

I closed my eyes as you smiled—
I knew then,
how the sky felt when it created horizons...

I enter the hallway, my skin dressed, my soul bare. I hear the keys hit the keyhole. Our eyes lock and a smile graces his face.

"Is that dress for me…," he asked, as he walked around me inspecting his newly scratched lottery ticket. I just smile and point to the kitchen.

"Lunch is ready, I made sure it was still hot…" but he had decided to alter the menu. Hands roaming over my silhouette, softened growls starting to do a mating call, he spun me around and kissed me deeply. I don't know what hit the floor quicker, the food or the clothes as I…

"Is that what you made for lunch…" my eyes pop open, daydreaming of what used to be fleeing the crime scene, leaving passion lifeless and cold on the floor of my heart.

"I thought I would change it up for you," I said, with a lower voice. "I figured maybe we could eat together, just for some time…"

Without even eye contact, he grabbed the food and opened the door, "I can't, you always act so needy and emotional. I come home for lunch, that should be enough and I need to get back." As he turned to leave, he looked at me, "Can you put a load of laundry in after your business meeting, it only takes a few minutes." The door shuts, and I stare down the hall into the laundry room, "they say the spin cycle works wonders…they say…"

I need a vacation from life, just a moment to authentically smile without having to do anything more—just a real smile, like I used to when we met throughout the day. The buzzer sounds and I toss in another load; sweats, me, and spin cycles…

— my soul is squeezing dried tears out in memories…

LOUNGING

You are my favorite couch of comfort
the kind you nestle into and let your essence fall—deeply into peace
the kind of forming that mold around the curves of my fears
and puts my courage at ease.

You are my favorite clothing of secure
the kind you wrap your vulnerabilities in
and watch safely fitting snuggly
the kind that you pull over the head of your strength
and falls effortlessly into a smile.

You are my favorite sunlight to awaken to
the kind of dawning that makes fantasies hunger
the kind of kiss that makes pleasant thirst
and imaginations lick wind—just in case it has been where you
have...

FORGED ♦ IN ♦ INK

Remember when life was simple—
check this box yes or no,
then taunt the boy/girl you liked—
sharing lunches, trading cards,
finding recess the highlight of the day—
until your crush walks by.

Where did the moments go…
why are we lost in the dark—
afraid to see stars in each other's eyes
settling for tone-deaf—
when the heart whispers
through moonlight…
What happened to feeling the skin of a soul
before a touch—the rush of chance
or
mind kissing lips,
because of anticipated thoughts.
Like the corner store candy shoppe,
taking your last,
just to get a piece of something so fulfilling—
the pleasure and excitement of cost.

Take me back to the innocence of 'meet'
touch my face with the feather of risk
take my pen into the hands of that passion…
write me into torn page corners—let me fall into the pockets of
your soul…

DOUBLE VISION

*Two, if by "see" the "eye" before **the me**,*
***the us** after **the we**—two if "bye" decree.*
One, if by become, the moment surrender has begun
chance circles until undone—courage takes on risk like a drunk
Merge, if by three— mind, soul, and legs with pleads
ink of tongue, with no resist—
paper penetrated, soaked into lined kiss.
"Too" if by you, doodling thoughts still untrue
wanderings into the wonder of new
—undeniable, the presence, you—do...

(Read bottom-up)

15

STRUCK

I've cried so hard in life,
that it burned the muscle memory
of fear into abs.

> *I've hesitated so deeply in my now,*
> *that it resuscitated the movement*
> *of my will.*

I've exhaled so sincerely in dreams,
that it exacerbated the lungs of my reality's self-control.
I've done so many things,
but none, so intensely as laying here,
a soul within a wick—
Wetly lit...

ANTICIPATION

Like the softness of worn shoes—you know, the kind that nestles the heel just right...
Or the first aroma of a brew
Makes a sound, just hitting the cup—intensely...
You are there.
Like, the simple inhale of a freshly opened window,
harmonies singing freedom amongst stagnation-yeah, like that...
You make my suffocation strip comfortable— breathing labored rhythms-deliciously.

> **You are home...**

PASSION & PERSPECTIVE

There is beauty in the
Simplistic...
Sunlight seems to just fall;
Yet to a seed,
it is a gentle candle—
A lantern, lighting the way for
Potential to fight through darkness

ASTROLOGY

I was never one to study signs
Until I looked into the universe called your eyes
And it was then that
the cosmos of my heart found my pulse—stargazing

DISNEY

I wonder,
if you ever understood,
I first noticed the moon gave light—
when you appeared.

   I wonder if you ever understood,
   I first realized the sun shines—
      when you spoke.

         I wonder if you ever understood,
            how you, Beauty—
      touched me, Beast, into existence.

I often dreamt of traveling to get away and breathe. I wanted to go somewhere beautiful, somewhere fragrance-free of hurt and sadness. I wanted to go somewhere lite and refreshing. Sadly, I could only go to my closet. So I built a fort within the space, my own personal Air-BNB away from life. I could retreat to the super host of my dreams and settle into the comfort of the exclusive suits...that is unless summoned.

GUST

Take me to a place where
things can be meant
set my desperation into ease
trace my soul
give my peace a breeze

DOUSED

I can still smell the aroma of your smile
as empty bottles of your touch,
still lie spilled, on the lap of my soul…

REASONS

You are like the first sight of frost,
as dry seasons end
the colors changing when the trees mature
the birthday song when the soul feels alive
the snuggles of sleeping until noon, after a rough path of life.

You are first sips of moments,
when you have forgotten how to dream
the candlelight burning in the darkness of demands
sometimes the classic song, when the ear needs a tune
my t-shirt and socks rocking, smile in groove

You are a head-on collision with hope's liberty
the passion of a pen when ink finds hand
the complicated sigh of feeling carefree
the beginning of sunrise where eclipse, had always been
—You are that is, purpose...

ETCH N SKETCH

Left breathless, like a lisp upon the lips still being tasted,
your words, like a Tsunami, pull my essence into a wave of yearning.
I find myself becoming blinded by the sunlight that envies your smile,
and yet, I surrender to the scorch your mind leaves—baffling touch...

If turbulence understood the sensation of your presence,
a breeze would have been renamed to a brisk puff,
If melody played a tune based on your voice,
harmony would cry in embarrassment—
learning it was always out of tune...

Sipping knowledge gained in the world,
wisdom becomes nothing but scorched taste buds—
listening to you speak.
But alas, "I am just thinking out loud"
*said, fingertips of smiles—recalling this pen tracing your **Hello**...*

SUCCUMB

Caramel kisses do send my way,
melt me like fire, forged by the heat of ignite
mold me like
many times, before
and even after the thousandth has hit
I won't ever tire of melting into your kiss

BRANDED

Don't go away, draw me in deeper
turn the touch I knew into ashes
and make my soul owned

FORGED ♦ IN ♦ INK

I used to envy,
the way the sky held the shimmer of the stars—so intensely
then I looked into your eyes,
and realized it had cheap imitations.

I often marveled at the waves,
the way the shores and crash knew just how to hold each other—
leaving memoirs of each moment formed as one,
then I heard the strength of your whisper and realized their passion,
was, but a faucet splatter.

I sometimes sigh,
finding jealously of the way the leaves trust the serenade of the wind
following without question into the unknown heat of a moment
then I felt the presence of your silhouette,
as,
my void hungered for the kiss of your shadow
to raise my soul like a white flag...

GLANCES

There is a gentle about you
Like a calming eye within
the mind's storm—a steady peace,
insulating my fragile and rocking my intrepid

There is a safe about you
Like faithfulness of shores
Devoted to reluctance of waves—
Never budging from fear's crash,
 leaving tokens of your foundation in my essence

There is a pause about your voice
Like a soothing breeze across
The skin of redundancy—a balm for the patchy and callous soul,
dry from unreciprocated efforts

There are moments when the night sky
shares anticipation of your presence
and
 I'm reminded of the illumination of your laugh—
Like shooting stars enthralled following where you last looked up
        — I too, am in awe with the horizon called your eyes...

FORGED ◆ IN ◆ INK

Mirrors have a way of reflecting the replications of angles. Just as in
life, we have encounters that create indications,
the images captured are all about the angles.
Sometimes you come across moments known as people,
and their likeness fractures your mirror into beautiful pieces.

Echoes of moments that sing out to the ghost of your shyness.
I knew better than to you play with jagged glass,
but even the flesh wound of a temporary grasp
was like poetry signing an autograph.

Have you ever encountered a reflection
that left your eyesight blinded into clarity?
Such were the mirrors, that left my soul catching glimpses...

LEGACY

I could no more, stay away from you,
than the twinkle from the stars...
I could no more, deny your presence,
than the day holding hands with light...
I could no more, remain whole apart from you,
than the intimacy of gravity and earth...
I could do so many things—but discard
you give my meaning its birth...

TANGO

They say we danced,
but I...
I say we became a page of sheet music
re-introducing moments to love...

They say we danced,
but I...
I say we sang as a symbol of unified souls,
finally understanding the meaning of touch's voice box...

They say we danced,
but I...
*I say we changed **Destiny's** legacy,*
as our hearts swayed into hands
and our passion became hopes poetry...

Our moments say we danced,
but I...

REST

*Lay, the weary of your searching
down upon the pillow of our found.
Place the shaken pieces of your safe
into the cohesiveness of this peace.
Run, the fingers of your caution's lust
through my trust of dedication's satiation.
Guide the untouched lips of your hope
into the soft kiss of mutuality—us.*

TOTAL ECLIPSE

*You could make the sun itself
long to wear flesh—
just so it can be near...*

A WHIRLED WIN

How did you, get here—
here, within my soul
unlocking within my release
gathering how I breathe
whispering into my strength; begin.

How did you get here—
here, beneath cries guard
silencing the rattling chains of past
breaking the law of pride's gravity
rocking my vulnerability into a
sweet lullaby of safety.

"How did you get here..."
asked the winds of my soul,
carried by a hurricane
masked as your smile...

Before you,
just ordinary blank pages lying...
So willing,
Like sheets eager to spread across the mind,
Heart's ink awaits, vision between life's commas...

ERECTED

Like innovative greatness,
the likes of which, have conquered odds in times before...
Brilliance awaits to be imprinted on the soul like architecture

...Tear down these remains...
...Erect an edifice...

...For here the testimony of your work provide skillful dexterity of
transcendence,
through smile—
my lines long to be
my curves mold in anticipation
my infrastructure boldly yearns
... to become, your blueprint...

ARTISTRY

You were a gentle beauty
Like ink breathing sunlight
Only to smile and make sunsets exhale

COLORED

Take me away to the breeze that is you,
keeping safe the evidence of your truth
you don't have to worry if I can handle the call
just gift me safety in each moment fear falls

Doing things that no one has
causing smiles that seal the door of the last
patiently learning the strokes of my smile
painting the canvas of haven with each day that pass

BED REST

your arms became pillows of safety
and understanding
as my wanderings closed their eyes
I lied down
and sighed into rest

TWISTED

What,
are you doing to my sanity…
Why,
do you have a choke hold on my caution…

GEOGRAPHY

You set the tone of how freely I can be,
speaking to my hidden—giving patient symphony.
So comfortable with uncomfortable,
this touch called your ease—I hear your lyrics,
they call, making me into melodies.
I can feel the pages turning, penning my skin.
My soul is becoming open,
like a book,
you crease my ends.

I thought about it, this smudge mark, we call possibly you and me—
replayed my reasons for running,
but they all lead me right to thee.
It would seem,
as a matter of fact,
that whichever road I take
still creates you as the map.

INTERTWINED

Walk with my essence and I shall encompass yours…
Touch my heart's mind until
my thoughts are dedications that
propel you—not into a moment,
but, into your purpose…
Within this mind I see,
that the answer to me is not you,
but "us"
and the answer to you,
is not me but "our"…

For this walk is more than just a journey,
it is transportation into evolution—
Past minds,
engaging present surrenders,
as one, inhaled, future soul…

REMBRANDT

Make a wish upon my star,
Show me the shadows that sing to your harms
Allow my essence to paint in the dark
I am touch— they left crayons, I form art

Take the canvas blackened from despair,
No rush to light the color, the work shows I care
I'll walk the corridors designed by night
Blindfolds by choice, my will have caught sight

Midnight blue or darkest of gray,
To the black hole called a soul
Or the sunrise called your name
No matter the moment, for you I can exist
Just waiting for the whisper,
I've already granted your smile, yes.

FALLEN ANGEL

Heaven can wait,
let's get all we need to do or say
Throw the apprehensions to the winds of time
and fall into the abyss called each other's mind.

JOUSTING

I've drug around enough shadows
and have a showcase, full of claws from every fight
I've low crawled through enough dungeons
to be reminded of the stench of limits
A simple trophy of remembrance,
that even a knight in shining armor,
needs a safe place to reveal a **soul**—*full of dents.*

KEYS

Do not knock and pound upon a door you never intend to enter
Do not throw rocks of passion at windows you have not the courage
to break

Do not take the last drink of sorrow
if you do not plan to refill hope's cup
Do not, I say…
This is not a wish upon a well of stars
And then content, stay wondering where they are
Do not make me call you the moon
if I will not be the sky
If you cannot look at my presence without hellbent in the eye
Nor, count the moment—soul holding out hand
Let it be as a vice grip for keeps, not fear still raging in war—
*like a **General**, holding reigns of command...*

XENA

Been the damsel and pressed through distress,
fought off dragons and vested beast
understood in all the moments, that even a heroine
seeks a moment to find peace

WIZARD

Smoke screens and mirrors,
I have no need of, with you…
More potent, than moonlight drinking liquor—
I find my soul, eclipsed by the view.

Forebodings are memories,
lit, quicker, than an arsonist…
Take my storm, into your quiet—
torrential downpours, seem like a kiss.

Smiles spinning more rapid, than
Dorothy calling for Toto, in-flight
you got this drawing—hesitations following,
Yellow Brick Bright.

STRIPPED

You are all the comforts of home
and the tumultuous thrill of a voyage
The familiar scent of a favorite meal
and the aftertaste of cravings seared on the soul's taste buds

The slow pace of a good ole' rocking chair
and the crash of gravity kissing caution into surrender
The shades of refreshed gracing on the skin
and the racing tongues of sweat dripping from thoughts conversing

You are the shape I didn't see coming
and the mold that I've folded my exhale into
So many things I overheard the clothes of my vulnerability say
as they whispered "yes" crumpled on the mind's floor...

DIVE

Like rivers that run deep, you have turned
the trickle of my curiosity into flowing cascades of want and
surrender
— navigate me,
until our willpower drowns in the tsunami of oneness called
Us…

HEAVENLIES

You can be,
the sun or the moon
As long as I can be,
your sky

GROUPIE

What do I want to say
to you, to us, to me?

How do I simply convey
you're this, my that, now free?

When can I whisper my name,
in your soul, on your tongue,
through your smile—I'm just wondering…
sighed this single glance,
blended amongst the crowds.

MONSTER INK

Have you ever looked into the eye of a storm so intensely beautiful
that your tears fainted
your pulse lost rhythm
your exhale became a coward
and all you could do was blink
until your shadow wept?
Yeah, those eyes are a catastrophe—
I "prey" for my destruction daily

ECHOED

Here we stand, offerings of trust
learning how to grow as embers of choice.
Connecting all the moments that remain hidden—by souls
who had become buried treasure maps from rejection

But just as fate catches sight of a shooting star,
like stolen moments between the ocean and moon—
glances exchange tidal waves
suddenly, unspoken is more articulate than a voice.

PROMINENCE

There are marks within these marks, that my soul does wear
hurt and pains forged as skin—
a struggle, damned to keeping them from clothing my dreams.

I sit often within reflections as jagged glass
broken promises shipwrecked into shattered breathing—
my will on a ventilator, longing for trust's oxygen to inhale.

But sometimes, in the stillness of the night,
in the midst of my struggles and low crawls toward courage,
I see a star burning by candlelight.

How did this come to be, you,
a mere shadow of beauty and strength, scarred into each,
would kiss my restoration into admiration with seals...

SUBDUED

Let me express the essence of your song—
my soul longs to give mastery
tune...

Let me bestow at your feet,
the original artwork that your presence
has painted upon my heartbeat...

Let me shine in your sparkle,
my diamond "mind"
for in it, priceless gems of
"real" await excavation...

If I told you,
if I showed you...
Oh,
how you are my completions
perfume of choice; every day...
No rehab can cure.
No medication can correct.
Submission—
you made strength
   blush, learning yours...

BALM

Let me be the healing balm to the scars of your life—
restoration that refills the fountain of trust's youth
rejuvenation of wisdom that was long lost to age

Let me be the emotional palate—
turning famished hopes and letdowns
into plates for safety's gluttony

Let me be shores—
sands gifting pieces of my foundation
taken like grains of glitter, adorning waves of your crash

Let me be—
many things in the night or in the light
only let me be,
this simple—

reclaiming...

GENERATIONS

He said we should have been born old
where the gift of stories was left to behold—
then the moment of legacy a mark would leave,
as generations learned the courage of free.
Living and learning save kisses of sin,
*and eventually left this life as children—**Pure**.*

He told of why life is "backward" rattles;
how the moments are actions of choices in shadows—
that the end result is just a shifting floor,
and the pursuit of all, just a revolving door.
There is a rhythm, and strength to that,
*the selfless act of coming into knack—**Acceptance**.*

So, I sat in silence, and pondered within,
the truth he spoke and the reasons I lived—
like raindrops falling into the soul,
flood gates of understanding drowned my know.
The wisdom of ancients come and gone,
*sunsets and rises of choices now done—**Effort**.*

Now before you sit blueprints and seasons,
fears and faith like a lighthouse of reasons—
as the waves of growth and tides unknown,
navigate the journey of a soul searching for a home.
The heart will always speak in a whispered demur,
*given enough reason to find time or comfort—**Rebirth**.*

FROST BITE

You are my sun
giving serenade to the shivering skin of my life
—take this hypothermia-stricken passion
And
thaw my essence

LUCK

My heart is in it…
I could cope if it was just a moment—temporary infatuation,
a chance inhale of your smile's fragrance
But my heart is in…
Now, you are a part of my soul—
to be memory or love's legacy, either way…
*My heart is in it… **damn***

PLEDGE

I'm addicted to the real of you...
Through the fire,
hanging intertwined within heart and wire,
all the moments in-between,
this life we can do like an Olympic team
I took an oath within my whisper
Promised to love unto life with relentless tender
I do not know just how or why,
But I'm willing to find out for the rest of our lives...

DELIVERY

This wine of the mind, the alcohol of sobriety—always inebriating the guards that stand post at my heart's gates...I often hate them, the weakness of their tattered and battered armor— always dropping the drawbridge of my resistance to the rawness of expansion.

Tracing the beauty of words with the fingertips of my soul, before the click ever said hello...

I would sit and gaze for hours at the dawn they created in my mind's horizons. I would stretch out on the petals of softness that those delicately placed thoughts would give while swirling the tip of my toes into the cooling warmth of your pen's cascades. I would sob hysterically with emptiness and pass the bottle of rejection back and forth between me and the sadness I had decided to have a one-night stand with...

I tried to casually thumb through your lines, but the clothing of my soul would get caught- snared by threads that had unraveled against the sharp edges of realness with yet a tender poise; I would often leave shreds of my soul's garments like breadcrumbs, scattered by the winds of curiosity and hesitation...

Like a dehydrated deer, panting at brooks of water, I was paralyzed at the thought of sipping the sweetness of bitter reminders of love and pleasure- the hope and understanding that I no longer believed I could digest...Even now, finding food for others, carrying life water to the thirst of depleted, while I am anorexic... Always anorexic...

cont'd

51

It is as if my daily meals consist of wishing, hoping, praying, and being prepped for a meal no one intends on cooking—too much for many, always enough for all—I live as an unwrapped present amongst the cries of people, screaming for the evidence that gifts exist...

Pull the ribbon of these eyes—they see you.

SECONDHAND HEARTS

A rummage sale
Of collectible plights
Scraps of promises
Ashes of dreams
Empty picture frames of
What should have been
Pieces of materials left from
Souls
Glitter now useless
trapped in pockets as fake gold
Still, they hope to be sewn
by a hand and bond
To become a tapestry to be hung
In a heart ready to be stitched, insignia marked loved

INFUSED

Like, water tasting the lips
of lightning
or the desert sands
feeling the first caress of a raindrop

Like, the summer heat falling in love
with the swaying hips of a breeze
or moonlight, awestruck
over an individual reflection

Like, sunsets presenting a throne to midnight as queen
or breaking dawn
leaving love bites, on the parting nape of night—
still in a sweet slumber

You have become exhales
teaching strength, the passcode to enter this body
Now pauses seek to inhale you
like a beggar,
as fear leaves the mind

Like, a moment in time
can become a series of legacies,
turn each page of destiny deliberately—
but only if you can
read me like a signature card.
—Autographed body and soul

ORBIT

I would travel through the seven seas,
just to orbit around a moment of your smile.
I could journey beyond the world and back,
just to witness the symphony, that is your mind.

I would take a beating like the windowpane—midsummer day,
if it meant, I could bask in the shadow of your peace.
I would gift my soul to the winds,
if it meant, I could have a moment that eases how you breathe.

I would shut out all the colors that make the day,
so your touch could paint my sight.
I would flatline my will and its caution,
just to encounter the trust of your surrender's moonlight...

WHITE

You are a war
I would gladly stand on the front lines for,
If it meant, I would bleed into existing...

ALWAYS

Just as the clouds leave fingerprints across the back of the sky
And the sun tenderly sips from the skin it tastes
Like the moon holds hands with the stroke of midnight
And the ocean's addictions draw from the shore with repetitious hits
You have become like sand filling the desert of my thoughts
Like cracks of joy shifting the fault lines of my inspiration's
foundations
I could bask in the moment— even if it was just one,
But I'd rather you be, my one life stand

TRACED

I've been around paper machetes masking as crowns
And puppet masters with an arsenal of gold platted, strings
Watched open skies through cellophane-colored promises
And listened to hopelessness sing like wind chimes

But you have a serenade about your smile
And a peace that is nothing shy of a sunrise
Like morning dew finds the lips of a petal
And the air whispers delicately into the lungs—
I can see moments hemming the patterns of your silhouette into
tapestry—
Outlining my essence

INHALES

Sometimes I can't feel my inspiration—
My pen is drab
My paper parched
My hope, sleep-typing through life...
But every now and then,
The window of my courage rattles,
And I hear soul chimes,
singing me into existence with a breeze...

And just like that,
The sun breaks through
And I can smell the horizon—

A freshly poured cup of You

SHEET MUSIC

I could study under
Mozart
Bach
Or even
Tchaikovsky—
And still,
I'd uncover nothing composed with more enthrallment
than the sound of—Your presence...

58

TAINTED

He gave Rembrandt a lesson with a flick of his whisper
Created shooting stars with the lick of his mind
Colored my sight with the kiss of his gentle
Molded my exhale through the hands of his safe
Masterfully he drew me into heart's perfection,
staining my eternal with the pen of his, hello

REVITALIZED

You turned dark skies into golden horizons
Masking as silver linings
Take the cold showers of the world's spit
And
Turn it into cascades of waterfalls
Whipping around my worth's mountains
Just as despondency tried to dry the brooks of my hope
You brought the Sun of Seen out...

PIECES

You broke me…
You took the pieces of my hurt
Polished them into mosaic art
Blew winds of comfort upon the flames of fear
Turned it into a snowfall of faith drawing near
Dug trenches of hope —Doused my shame with acceptance to cope

Took me into hands
strong enough to scorch like the sun
But gentle enough to fall like dusk
to which I hungrily run
Oceans called eyes
that safely undress my scars
Like the corners of all the earth—
I want to be where you are

Be shores to your sands
Cans to your plans
Yes, to your forever—Addicted helplessly
to your trust and fervor
So, into your hands, I lie like a spade
*"You broke me, this hold…" whispered my former owner—**Afraid***

COVET

My yearning screams so intensely,
it has gone hoarse—yet even now,
it is shouting whispers.

I caught your scent on the match of my essence—a heat so devouring,
a flame should recant claiming torch.

You have permeated my thoughts so deeply,
that my mind calls you a wind chime—
and still...

Can you even understand,
the night shivers that these tears experience—
thoughts of undressing your trust.

In a sea of crowded experiences,
can you too,
feel stars forming constellations just so our silhouettes caress—
I will ask the moon, once it lets go of envy...

DAMPENED

Open, these rivers of wonderment run,
Clueless trickles of natural highs— fall.
The drought of genuine has found a season of change; you.
The spring—my hidden oasis.

Like the desert is in need and doesn't know about the rain,
Like the mountain peaks wait and then find hugs from a cloud,
Like the ocean's depth hoard the love of the shore—
Moments draw life
from the breath of your smile...

A stranger smiled,
and with that came this momentary train wreck of abandoned ecstasy
displacing my soul...

My boarding pass of destitution fell out of my pockets from the
collision and my struggles lie scattered around my feet like unclaimed
baggage. Like a conductor inspecting my boarding pass for
legitimacy, I instantly retrieved my ticket to reasoning, and in that
very moment,

> *I felt the sweat of uncertainty run down my spine...*

I hadn't assessed if my person had sustained any damage, but I could
feel a surge of energy building up momentum on the tracks of my
will's mind...

And without fearing the repercussion of impairment, I signaled for
help with all the strength I could find...

I smiled back...
and with that, the mirror announced help arriving at the station of—
> *deflected destitution...*

FORNICATIONS

She was a diary of ink,
Spilling hidden truths—
pages that lied upon the lied—
to, on, and with...

Read by the soul,
Heard by the heart,
Understood with the **Will**—
indeed such a dark art.

To the onlookers it was poetry,
To the muse, flattery—
For the house—a confirmed battery.

A hidden book,
conceived In the closet of secret ink,
Until the pages, heavy with burden,
Poured like loose leaf...

She was a diary of ink,
Spilling hidden truth—
pages upon pages of
Lies & Red Shoes.

Read and heard,
Seen and **Received**.

Recognizable to only—
A mirrored image of thee...

SAFE

How do I fall in you again
the past just seems to plagiarize
the moment eavesdropped on by coincidence
now being copywritten by hope and chance

How do I fall in "let's" just see
when the moments aren't hindered by fears that breathe
when time is of the essence and yet so are our pause
offerings of newness that hauntingly draw

How do I fall in quieting the storm
while soul clouds stop gathering of hesitations in downpours
while sunsets call out to paint with the color of our ignite
and you seem to be the artistry that gives my essence moonlight

How do I fall without making a sound
this crash is a whisper, yet the moment resounds
this hunger is insatiable yet I'm a glutton for your grin
and happily, I kiss with courage,
the lips of sin
let the fall begin...

FORGED ♦ IN ♦ INK

Now,
Somewhere, between the lies and truth,
The soul within ink broke…
Now pages become,
Nothing more than, discarded tissue
Of
Where I wiped my trust…
As I close mirrored reflections
And
Embrace the truth of thoughts
***ASHES** to **ASHES**, and safety to dust….*

ASHES

It's no good going on living in the ashes of a dead happiness.

◆◆◆

Nevil Shute

FORGED ♦ IN ♦ INK

Today I had a crying spell.|
It was as if my tears needed a coach; panting they longed.
Running a marathon down the skin of my memory, they jogged.
Dehydrated thoughts like sweat,
formed across the forehead of my senses—
as the winds of change blew through my will,
I could feel the inevitable—
"I'm full and need draining," screamed, the voice box of my lungs—
the exhales of my hope pained with laryngitis.
"Today, I had a crying spell," whispered, courage.
"I know," said, the beat to the heart, "so did we..."

*I lit the cigarette of my mind and took in one long drag. What the hell is **Marriage**?*

Was it the joining of two hearts that vow to beat as one? It should be, but the thought of that made my soul choke as I started coughing up the last bit of hope that had been wedged between my lungs. The problem with that is—some hearts vow to beat as one, while others hemorrhage.

I blew a ring of smoke into the air of thought as I looked down on the band that was as meaningful as the ashes of my trust falling to the ground. Marriage— when done right, was supposed to be a type of bliss that sets fire to desire, strength to weakness, stability to insanity, or so I have been told—At least that is what the magazine in my hand said.

*Yet, all I knew was the cold, unrelenting emptiness of broken promises, cheated out of dreams, dusty hopes, and flat lined passion of relationships across the board. I looked at the empty cigarette box called joyous memories and pondered a while longer— **Marriage, Family, Relationships**, the moment when covenant, bonding, mutuality are entered, and new beginnings have been formed. I must have found the wrong **Life Event** coordinator—this venue book so far was definitely about hits, but never misses.*

As I threw the last bud of my smile into the trash can and exhaled the smoke of safe into a fainting ring, I looked down again at the ban that symbolized unity— gold-plated, solitary confinement—if this was unity, I crave sedition.

cont'd

Running my fingers over the diamond, I understood, so much more, the cost of its luster— pressure and coal under relentlessness. I was still coal, wondering if I would ever see the diamond of my smile. As I turned to walk down the hall, I placed the box of the family album back on the shelf and closed the door to the closet that held my wedding gown. Spraying the air freshener of a smile and fixing the clothes of my heart posture, I looked at the doorknob one last time—

Behind that door lay the evidence of my marriage— stains of woe embroidered into wedding garments, while the garter of trust and hope strangled the movement of my safety within an inch of its life.

FORGED ✦ IN ✦ INK

These next few pages will not be pretty chapters.
These next few ink smudges will not be smiles and rainbows.
This will be the marriage of violence,
abuse,
abandonment,
and
fractured hope within relationships
on every echelon—some don't live to find the end of the story,
but when we do,
*we birth **Ashes** and make charcoal masterpieces...*

DESERT

Scavengers hunt for missing parts
Amongst vultures, named vulnerabilities
And desert lands called apprehensions—
Hearts reside like an oasis of undiscovered restoration
awaiting footprints that long to tread
 through the sands of complacency
Thirsting for a sip of reciprocity— real...

Dehydrated of trust
like a palm tree bending
there is a quench in cool tears, splashing hope—
Until the stumble comes
A sojourner seeking amnesty from choice's plight

Offering no mirage—
A nomad of belonging
Fortifying brick instead of tent,
with eyes that form a nation under surrender.

Flags waving of coat of arms
Music of belonging— playing invitation
If it is love,
 Let it read like a stain upon my soul
 But be patient, these fears,
These fears would rather it be a watercolor just passing through—
The safety of disappearing ink...

(now read it backwards)

MISTRESS

I was the side chick to your past,
The tissue you use, to overcome what didn't last...

The sink you use to wash hope's mask,
While checking for shadows that may be cast—
Upon the doorstep of your worth,
While giving wreckage all your girth...

And sometimes,
like a slot machine,
The lever is pulled—
And "won" is nothing more, than being a fool...

ASPHYXIA

I heard so loudly,
The throat of each
Raspy and Burning
unquenched flame of ink,
Like running through smoke, while out of breath
Tears spoke without roar
As paper caught smoke inhalation, while silently listening...

RIVALRY

Do not penalize me for the abandonment I was not present for...
For the atrocities of your heart—
crimes I never pulled the trigger on...

For rejections of promises,
You never gifted me to hold...

Stop leaving me as tear-stained causalities—
promises that went to war...

INCISIONS

I once wished so weakly upon a star
and
wondered if the words would be heard afar
I'd seal them silently with my tears
And wipe blood-stained offerings from my fears
I'd wait to see the dawn and light
But first swollen eyes must heal from
Plight
And as I sit, one black, the other blue
I'd sing with no voice box—
Is love ever true...

DESICCATED

One day, I'll stop casting,
Wishes into a desert—
Thinking my tears
Will be enough to cause,
A crack, to become an oasis...

TARNISHED

*I have been the "**Holy Grail** of **Love**"*
Things, people want,
None will pay for
The quest some seek—
None complete
The apparition that some sought
Vision none caught
The art of ash,
*Craving "**Unveil**"*
like a charcoal masterpiece
Yet here I sit,
Fainted traces of watercolor
On paper,
Resistant to anything but stains—

CEMETERY

How many ways can my soul break
My essence
My rise
My hope
How many ways can my tears drown
My heart
My smile
My trust

How many ways can I die with full lungs
My vulnerability
My surrender
My open

How many... I've lost count
Except the number of tombstones
That fill the graveyard of my love...

HEMORRHAGE

Collateral damage for charges other blew
The shrapnel of their disloyalty and antics
Speaking like a severed aorta—distrust
Actions speak louder than words
But only when one has something they know how to prove

DRESSED

Fumbling through life.
Answers come at the hellish of times.
Kindred minds reveal their deceit.
Essence of real overwhelmed with repugnant duplication.
Ambition is adventurous.
Solitude ain't gratitude.
Simple, Cashmere "sweaters".

(acrostic)

PROGENY

She was the stepchild of biological parents—abandonment's offspring
Unseen, even when role-call heard.
The holey sock, once favorite pair—
no longer family fashionable—worn; wore on, warred on.

The jewel of denial,
priceless crowned priced—less
heiress of slighted, yet regal.
The court jester,
*deemed **Court** of **Appeals**—or feels*
so the hierarchy taught; teacher.

Still, the blood right of worth
signed off on birth—legitimacy
claims clutching to identity's license.
Until the rights,
Phoenix of plights,
with ink-hearted knights; nights,
of the round table of rites—
writes...

FORGED ◆ IN ◆ INK

Love always seems to be just out of my grasp.
A mirage, a few steps away.
A delicate fragrance that floats by with an absence of scent—
What is this familiarity that aroused my consciousness,
but leaves me demented?
If I was just shattered,
I could live as mosaic art,
But my will is evaporated,
Before you is a corpse damned to breathe—
A fleeting image in the shadows.
Suffocating with a burning yearning—
embers within me I didn't know existed.
Gasping for a breath.
But my strength's lungs have collapsed—forever out of reach...

TEMPEST

When the winds of enough blow
Then you take cover
But the clouds were gathering
while your selfishness was
Basking in the sun of flattery

Rain drops of hardening fall
Now you look for dry shelter
But the downpour was swelling
while your arrogance was
Ignoring the humility of the air

No one pays attention
to the quiet before the storm—
They should

ENIGMA

Heart pumping through masking tape
Pulse racing from willpower's jumper cables
I sit trying to bring order to overturned
Trash cans in the middle of a typhoon—
Amazing how time and effort
becomes more delicate than wet tissue paper
As I lay like pieces on the floor of your exhale
A Jigsaw Puzzle

PARADOXES

Little Dark secret,
You're good for the bed
You silence the confusion,
that Fight in the head
Little Dark secret,
You make things right
You make pages tear,
Of when soul was in plight
Little Dark secret,
Masterpiece of behold
It's not my fault,
That you don't accept your role
While everything,
Old, broken and gone
Plays like a lullaby
That won't move on
Little Dark secret,
Sits tucked away
Good enough,
Just not for light of day.

SULLY

Do you see me, not the facade of the present—
Presented
But, the me covered in the ashes of rise—
The smile holding the open wounds of purpose,
A heart carrying the grenade of surrender,
still to be had.

Do you see me, not the silhouette of moments unlearned—
But, the pieces of tattered art taped together as mosaic—
The expression of screams wearing whisper
Like a crown,
A soul walking the streets of tangible,
banished from the bed of
Peace

Do you see me, I wonder as I speak—
While the keys of fingers type my soul
Leaving lipstick disgraces on the collar of
your paper...

WARNINGS—please understand, this is not to belittle, this is to free
— those who suffered like me, those who struggle like me, those who
never had a voice—like me

People often mistake the way I celebrate others and pour out as some
type of "positivity message" but it is more like, those who hand out
water during a marathon.

Many aren't familiar with my past and so they underestimate the
capacity my heart actually walks in. I'm not for the faint of heart!

I'm not for those who need cookie-cutter history and the virtuous
pristine; I am imperfectly perfected, grace!

I will never apologize for not caring if the cup is half full or empty,
but rather, if you thirst and how I may pour back to the capacity you
can handle.

A charming couple, her husband— the father of some of my siblings
—as I have siblings I share the same mom with, but they share the
same parents, and siblings I share the same father with— they too
share the same parents; I am uniquely designed as one of my kind.

The significance, picture the utter bliss I see on a mother's face— the
love radiating from her, the safety she seems to know and find
comfort in.

Maybe it is how she stands against him— like he is a pillar of
strength and courage—for her...her husband.

cont'd

I wonder how she knows trust and confidence in him—the way they seem to fit without separation of anything standing between their unity of oneness...

I sat for a moment and stared at this picture that showed up in my feed, the only one I have allowed myself to look at— nausea set in momentarily, along with the three deep breaths I had to take, and the intentional prayer I decided to offer while staring at it, until I started writing.

I think of my mother. A beautifully soft-spoken woman, non - confrontational, a beast in running businesses, hospitals, etc. She is one of the most brilliant minds I have ever encountered with poise and class that has you thinking you left royalty; I don't quite understand her way of loving me, but I suspect, it is there. I was lucky enough to watch her love everyone, else—a lesson I learned, loving everyone, else too—minus me.

Yet, here she stands, glowing from pure unadulterated love and devotion. I envy this!

I didn't have the luxury of knowing love or him as she did—does...

I knew beatings, torments, and rapes at his hand—ages 6-14. I knew dressing in closets because he was outside my window or taking showers fully clothed because he was standing outside the door cracking it open—once, she caught him once, but my mother is a gentle heart, she is not built for conflict, she believed whatever he said against her gut. I wanted to hate her for that, but instead, I had

cont'd

a yearning to protect the gentle she was—is. Against it all, my love for my mother never wavered, only my questions of why her love for me would often, almost always… lay like a casualty of war before the army of her husband's smile.

I didn't know her knight in shining armor, I knew relentless beatings and being dropped off as payment for whatever drug he wanted when we went on my "daddy-daughter dates" that always made my mother smile — her smile, even as an adult, still haunts me into wanting to preserve it at all costs. I suppose it will be forever lost now, but it is an exchange I must pay to redeem my own.

When he finally went away, my mother, nor his family, could ever come to terms with losing, "her husband, father of her kids, precious innocent son, uncle, brother…" as it was put "a loss that certainly superseded anything I experienced…" There would always be a wall between us, an invisible disregard for me as a daughter outside of the shadows. I have always watched her, always so tenderly trusting of him, as he would paint me however when she left for work or school, she would accept no questions asked— as a beautifully trusting spouse and parent would do. His family would begin to say things in our brief interactions like "I'm praying for you, I hope you get help soon…" I appreciated the prayers, I really did, but the help, you should have invested that help in a Groupon coupon in that unsavory flesh you call "kin" and stopped victim shaming— because you, not I, could not come to terms with the monster you unleashed into the earth.

cont'd

I learned then, that unhealthy knack of preference for others, over my well-being, preference for those who would assault my sanity and innocence, love, and devotion—something I'm free of now and help others choose to heal in.

But God must have taken special care in the silver linings HE would place in my life.

My mom met and married the man I know as daddy when I was 15 1/2 and he taught me not all men hurt and brought a safety I had never known into my life. He would go on to pamper her, and still love on me and all my siblings even when he pulled 16 hr shifts— something about his stability to always come back, that will always be something I adored and have the utmost respect for. To me, any man (in this case my daddy), who comes into a ready-made family and pours out with all his heart and soul for their betterment is a crown.

After almost 20 yrs of marriage, my mom divorced my daddy and remarried my tormentor, abuser, rapist, thief, and finally stepfather, after the love of my life - my grandmother passed. My entire family(all aunts, uncles, cousins, and siblings) on my mother's side (save my second to youngest brother and one cousin) didn't know what to do and didn't want to be in the "middle" and proceeded to ostracized and not speak a word to my children and me, welcome him back into the family, and take their "truth" to keep the peace for the last decade or so until I saw them a few years ago...

cont'd

During that time, I was left in an abusive marriage in all aspects for two decades until I realized it was not my job to help him get better— I'd leave, him, all we had, all I built, all I knew, and drag my younger three to a state I knew nothing about and no one. I've never been afraid to risk, had to learn I was in domestic violence— since I'm a fighter and didn't see myself as a battered woman. I have never seen myself as a victim of anything EXCEPT— not knowing a reciprocal heart posture when it comes to love. Spent the last 8 yrs. learning what it means to be a compliment to a person, not completion, and how to pick from wholeness, not voids.

About two years ago, I sat with my mom and stepfather, and for an entire week, I showed loved and forgiveness, and honor— I honored them as parents without either of them acknowledging, admitting, or asking for forgiveness — they won't. He will never own up to it and my mother, to protect the fragile heart she is and gives, had to convince herself that it was a lie made up by a very disturbed young girl. But, I don't need either of them to do that—apologize, I am strong enough to cover them even though their job was to cover me.

I am strength where none is present and it's okay— I will never judge the wife in her, as I was not his wife. I will not judge the mother in her, as I was not her mother — even now, my heart aches for the pain she might feel from these words and the shadow they might cast upon her. I don't want that for her, but I can't deny being a voice for those who always live in "what happens in this house, stays in this house syndrome" and more. I must be the example I share with others. I want to be this example— no scratch that, I must be—so that my

cont'd

children and the lives I touch, can never say they didn't see or experience the love of one of CHRIST's relatives, trying to reflect HIM in a world that does so poorly and so relentlessly bad of it. But please be clear, not the religion of HIM—that mess hurts and I'm sorry for those who have been subject to that mockery. In the relationship of HIM, you can be well versed on a subject and not know the heart of the matter; sadly, most are well versed, but haven't a clue of HIS heart —know I am so sorry for those moments and the damage it caused. Now, some may be reading and I'm thinking (ey, that isn't your thing) I won't knock what works for you, do the same for me, yeah...

The real impact of that love causes you to know you are not the child, girl, or woman who was broken, but whole. I am whole and restored; a gift for the man coming into my life who deserves to experience wholeness without penalty for atrocities he never committed against me.

My future, may you always know, that when I love, I love having pushed through, crawled past, pulled myself up, and dusted off, all of that and some I will not say for those to tender (it's okay, I'm good— really) to prefer, venerate, admonish, admire, desire, honor, respect, deeply love, and be devoted to you (1peter 3 AMP).

That when I say I got you, I got you with elbow grease, hair tie, and knee pads for the trenches we gotta dig in, crawl through, and rise above—that I did this without women teaching me what to do except three mothers showing me at different stages, what a wife looks and loves like...

cont'd

I didn't share this to humiliate my mother or family - I recently reconnected with my biological father's side of the family and they were unaware; I suspect they will have questions and emotions — I'm good, I wanted you to see what I have become before you had to see what I stripped off and for you to understand why I call and love my dad, as dad— he stayed!

He had no reason or obligation to stay and he did, for me and my children and theirs.

I look at my mom and I am so happy to see her glowing— in love! I respect she followed her heart and although I could not do that, I understand it was her truth and her life. I love her and, in my heart, I fight to honor the title she carries, even if I have to not have her presence in my life the way traditionally, others get to enjoy— restoration doesn't always mean they will be in your life without limits, or all together.

It is painful every day— rise and slumber, work my ass off, mother, and friend without the security of having the presence of a mom...

I shared this so people will understand, I'm not fake when I show me — I been a crown, I been shoe prints, I been Jezebel in red bottom shoes and no underwear, I been, many things... now I'm just trying to be soap and water for my soul. It cost me to be this heart and although it is not "I am She-Ra" in appearance, I am the epitome of all things strong, loving, sacrificial, and real in a whisper most times and a thunder when required.

Live your life. Heal because you deserve to heal. Give experiences a page, but never your biography— Expect in and with tears, but never settle; you have the right to reclaim you ♥

A MOTHERLESS CHILD

I am a motherless child
The orphaned hand print of love withheld
Nurture and protection
Yeah, estranged siblings
Like the family reunion my peace never attends

I am a motherless girl
Packaged abandonment
the broom closet of Lost and disheveled
A room of discarded
Dreams and Innocence

I am a motherless teen
Imprinted image of Battered and tattered
shards of broken
forming skin to shelter
While the winds of withheld blow

I am a motherless woman
Perfumed in dingy
Clothed in afterthoughts
Sitting in the darkness of
Shattered
Awaiting the crumpled pages of
this ridiculed soul to finally read
Like fresh air

Decency, you left me motherless

BLUDGEON

Tear-stained hollers rolled down my face—
reckoning escaped in dry heaves
It was not my pain yelling at the top of its lungs—
But my heart,
Clinging with bloody fingertips to drums—
daring my heart to awaken the beat again...

OBEDIENCE

He had a hunger in his eyes
A rugged strength
I was the object he set his affection
and my composure didn't understand
programmed for command
succumb to demand
all I knew was how to
be the slave—of conditioned

HOCUS POCUS

Lure of disposable ink
Playing games with paper and winks
Careful to not mix their batch
Not knowing they trying to fool a match
Woven lures in splatter
Character shown in chatter
But I guess we are enrolling in school
And it's back to the drawing board like a fool
Lines are arson you see
They set ablaze, fervor or fury in free
So be careful how you stain heart pages
Some of us are an incarnation that's immune to sages

CALL

I thirst for the simplicity of drought,
the utter drying up of this well, I call love—
for these hard, cracked surfaces of cynicism,
to emerge through the soft ground of optimism.
I long for the blistering winds of bitterness to blow,
instead,
this cooling mist—drops of understanding relentlessly
trickle down my sweating heart.

I whisper to the vultures, hoping of vulgarity to soar,
the eating up of all the flesh of my compassion
the draining of these sacrificial veins—
might and fight giving blood no more in a transfusion.

I would that I could lie down in defeat,
refusing the mantra of low crawl to the oasis of resolve
drawing a last breath of commitment to overcome in soul
instead,
I again, gift the wings of white flags
surrendering to dreams dancing across
desert-like rolling clouds—watering tumbleweeds...

GRETEL

The age of innocence when life meets light
And hopes pick sunflowers
And dreams play hopscotch
Where laughter is wallpaper
And trust is windows
I must have taken a wrong turn
Following cardboard cutout breadcrumbs…

MOTHER GOOSE

I was six years old when I learned how to watch tv
and play a game sideways
"you watch cartoons, and I will tickle you,
we can play hide and seek…"
But I never found my funny bone in that spot,

my cousins…

Maybe you didn't know how to play anymore,
I mean, after all, you were 16
Maybe that is why you asked your twin, to come and help you believe

I still wonder what you were hiding, while my innocence
Waited for the seek…

COSTUMES

She was a fun friend, I eight, she 14,
We, the perfect dressed-up belles
She would wanna play family, and roles be assigned
I was impressed, dual characters I could play on a dime
But she always wanted to be a husband
and welp, he needed a wife anyways
And you would say "this is normal, to practice so soon...
Hold still and just relax,
we can have lunch it will be ready by noon..."

And I would trust my friend because after all,
we were perfect dressed up belles
Eating lunch and watching cartoons
But always first, the strip tease of my jukebox—
a family tune...

THERAPY

She took notes on my childhood
Offered tissue for the pain
Listened intensely to the heartache
And cried endlessly at my soul stains
Then the buzzer would go off
And the moment would end
She had paid for the role
And now she was through
She was a nurturer and was comforting
Even when it was my turn to cry
She would stroke my hair and promise it would end quickly
But I knew it was a lie
She kept whispering she loved me
And I tried to play deaf
She was always affectionate
Said it would set me free
After all, the therapist knew better
She, just another pimp, vying for keeps…

FRAGILE

The things I will do to you, you will learn to enjoy
The things I will grow you into, you will learn to embrace
The way you will surrender when I call for you,
you will learn to love—Me,
You will learn to love me, as I fell in love with you at first sight
My own "glass menagerie" she called me
I will be gentle until I'm not, but for now,
let's see what my money has bought
And like that,
my voice continued to be lost at the hands of one who lied to care
As I was branded into heavy trafficking of innocence away

INFERNO

Your touch left my soul singed...
My will—
a canvas charred—brushstrokes of your mind kiss me into ashes.
All that is left of my essence, a mural—
the reflection of our surrender
Shaming Fire...

SHARPSHOOTER

You are an unmarked bullet
With perfect aim
Once you've become the target
Surrender feels no shame
Expert shot, with immaculate kills
The kind of trigger finger that turns
death into thrills

A mysterious hat is worn over the heart
With a badge of soul shielded till just after dark
Smooth operator with sultry wind beneath the smile
A kill shot of beauty—hunger moaning in denial
Marksmanship you prayed would end you in bliss
As the smoke from the pistol
Tongued like a kiss
No novice to knowing which weapon of choice

But an assassin to composure just with spoken voice
At first glance, you would think "bolsters of know"
But the gun in the holster lets gentleness show
Tasting demise, you will plead your case
Many have died from beholding such face

Plenty have fallen to knees with the
Gesture in command
Now the bounty has doubled for the price of my demand
So, I sit, and I spin
The chamber into rounds
Playing Russian Roulette with passion's bullet—I found...

ADULTHOOD

Please don't go away from me,
said the memory to my heart...
Please don't let the moment I'm growing into,
tear our bond apart...

Please don't lose your shape,
the way that we just fit—
I'm trying to remember how you sang hello,
with every moment missed.

Please keep talking to the sun and telling it to shine,
Please keep forming clouds into shapes—
you know, the ones I like.

I guess I can keep sharing too,
I see you watch me still.
You use my favorite color in the sky,
from all the tears I spill.

TOUCHED

We sat face to face—
So much had been said,
so little spoken.
A **Master** of **Communication**,
Mentoring me in areas
deemed hearing impaired—
Pain...

REPUTE

It's like you're double-faced in soul and might
One side loves the other side fights
Twin flames, one of want the other of grief
And yet, both chase the soul of pleas
Which are you
Here or gone
Tell me what you want or let me go on
Will we call freedom a renegade
Or will you surrender to past mistakes made
I'm waving flags of red, white, and me
Fight for us or let me die free...

VAGRANT

You don't see,
the blood-soaked bandages that mount in heaps
from this soul—
the band-aids that fail as bands of aid,
unable to cover disappointment's ricocheting, bullet wounds.
The ear doesn't hear,
the loud whimpers of trust limping—
shallow breathing of a heart-searching its lung for one strong beat.

The smile can often hide,
courage living in leap years
and
dreams waiting for a sunrise, while chained to a total eclipse.

There are wounds hemorrhaging under the armor of expectancy,
coagulating into preservation,
waiting for purpose to cauterize.
No,
you don't always see what it takes to push through life in prosthetics
of encouragement—
But that doesn't mean, that this soul doesn't know, the Anarchy of
being—
displaced ribs of hope...

TONE DEAF

Wake me up inside
give me breath that causes life
set me free to see
that there is more than hiding or playing seek
Wake the rise I plead
tell me what you need
call into the deep
break the dame of bleak
I'm pounding on the walls
I'm gasping as I call
I am a fire that has wept
with flood gates of love in its depths
some play a simple tune
that lure most into sleepwalking blues....

TRAVESTY

If we are honest with ourselves,
we know how a person sees us,
we just have a hard time choosing to accept
what that person has shown our reflection to be—
learn to love you...

How many times, I found myself, making meals from crumbs—making do with leftover investments, while my tank ran depleted from filling up theirs. Why I justified the lack of what I deserved with motivational talks in my mind of "they only need time...then they will see..." I will never understand. I had to learn, to unlearn the broken in me in hands of abuse and misuse by anyone who ever said, "I love you" Except for a few here or there. A diamond, is still a diamond, even in a pig-sty—but it can't be appreciated or treated as one, while there...

GAMBLE

Friendship turned into chemistry labs
Trust becoming new soul DNA strands
Humility, understanding honor, is about sacrifice
Risk kissing dice, calling it the gamble of learning life
To what may come, the bliss of chance
To what has been, lessons in circumstance
And now we sit as a hypothesis of next
Such is love, in happenstance

SPLATTER

I thought you my paintbrush—
My soul
A canvas of your thrill
But now I know what you are—
fake love's wrist stroke
and I, a discarded color wheel

As long as self-value is a sliding variable,
we will never be balanced in how we see and appreciate ourselves.
It is hard to accept that someone you loved is no longer for you,
but that does not mean
That we shouldn't…
The truth is, they see you and what you offered,
they offered what they valued—It is just hard to accept,
reflections.

FURY

While you shattered safety with selfishness of ego—
humility swept up shards of us,
with the heart's bare feet...

Madder...
My peace loved you—
while I slit the wrist of my transparency open,
you let trust hemorrhage—
applying first aid to every new smile...

Maddening...
Compassion breathed life into your existence—
As self-worth flared attention,
It was there, that hope's life raft
*Rescued **You**,*
only to leave, a gulping me...

Rage...
These screaming, silent teardrops,
falling from failed promises, into appreciations drought—
Since now, expectations hide stains
of the amnesia of me—

That is where I am at this point—I'm just spilling tears in ink, unsure
of what each drop holds except, that they splash like the color of my
soul, and I'm getting comfortable in this SKIN—
now learning to embrace my NAKED...

N A K E D

How much has to be explored and discarded
before reaching the naked flesh of feeling.

Claude Debussy

BARE

Keep on peeling my soul back with ink…
I will have your peace naked and panting
Keep on stripping my hesitations with gentleness
I will have your courage choking on fire
Keep on taking me to the brink of safe
I will have your legacy calling my love— grace

STRUCK

He fucked like lightning
And my soul
became his perfect storm

In the journey of the self, you soon discover likes and dislikes. The catalyst of each depends on what you are facing. That sounded so good to my mind, as I hooked the garments that had been lying over the chair. Slicking my hair back into a ponytail and grabbing my shoes, I left without a word.

"No point in establishing what you aren't there for," I thought. Get in, get on, get out, and business as usual. Life had taught me how to be a solider, marriage had taught me how to be a prostitute, and hurt had birthed me into a flame—a raging inferno and I was about to set shit ablaze. As I climbed into my car and adjusted my seat, I caught sight of him, her, them, peering over the balcony of my memories. Life had given me 50 shades of Whites, Grays, Blacks, and Blues... now, I had the crayon box and I was playing with the color RED...

I turned the engine on, but it didn't quite purr as well as my body had been trained to do.

The AC felt good against my thighs as I set my tunes and peeled down the street. Air always hits you different when you have nothing on underneath the clothes of your soul—and I was, head to toe, NAKED and unashamed...

CREATION

Enter me said my mind
My arch crying to be etched into your ancestry
With each stroke, we slayed denial's gravity
As he took my body like sunlight snatches darkness
I moaned like morning birthing a horizon

INKED

I want to put you on
Like a favored suit
Wearing your touch like lace
I kiss your presence into pages— crisp like an erection
I run you across the lips of my thoughts
As I tongue you into ink

TANGIBLE

I wish to tell you a secret, upon the soul of your lips
and leave coding as trails of goosebumps,
upon this hunger—called your skin.

Singing of desire, into the essence of a revived smile
stripping your trepidations,
after acceptance has tongued your safety—yet a while.

Inhaling you into passions of oxygen, until fear has lost its breath
and arching you into such peace,
that makes even your ancestors grin.

Unbridled and famished, my plan to leave your will.
I'm not a taste for the faint of heart
my flavor—for the real...

ACHE

Come lie with me behind the veil,
lift up the camisole of hesitations and setbacks

Come lie with me behind the fear,
shift the sheets of pretense and abandonment

Come lie with me behind the unspoken
dampen the moments with the sweat of trust

Come lie with me, here,
behind the ink—where we can wear heartbeats and pause

Until then,
I will wear the strength of your quiet
and spray your whispers—
        like the morning wears dew

DITTY

Sing to me, poetry,
Of fears and pleads
No need of shame,
I've been a devil in life's game.

Yet, ears to hear,
The soul of your pen—
A pied piper, piping…
Strumming these pages within.

Tis unkind, the melody of ink,
Spilling across my lines,
Leave my binding weak.
So, I rip them out,
One page at a time,
But, they fall like my clothing
With every inked rhyme.

Piled on the floor,
Words read as if you knew,
My body wears your pen,
Like a freshly etched tattoo –
Things you don't say,
But, say through silent doors,
Have formed sheets on my willpower—
loosing at seductions' wars...

VORACIOUS

My mind tried to taste you
Like a sample—
But my soul inhaled you
and now
My surrender is greedy…

DESOLATIONS

Your touch,
the most intense natural disaster
to hit my arch's Richter scale
Shook,
my willpower,
now lying-in ruins…

RENDERED

You could kill me
a thousand times over in one moment of silence...
Yet revive me within a second
with just a simple touch...

Some stroke the ego,
some the flesh...
Some
Well, they even caress the mind...
But none has ever been,
seduction
The pure serenade of...
This soul—until now

SEAMSTRESS

So here I lie, as Naked gratitude
Awaiting the moment when your frame
Drapes the arching of mine
And exhales of belief, fall like threads—
Unraveled

BATHED

Such an enigmatic inhale you are.
I can't keep my soul off you.
It is as if time found a loophole of how to capture your brilliance—
And only dawn's light,
        Bold enough to emulate.

                Moon runs its fingertips like a nightlight for the sky,
                        As presence so thrust so deep within my walls
                My shadow developed fingerprints scratching.
                                Confidence in excellence—
                        Thundering whispers of relaxation.

You are a gift in moments,
the petals of my lip's flower, opening to raindrops you drip
enthrallment is now dancing into puddles igniting—
        making even a flame sweat...

PERMANENT

State lines between us
17 years of being thus,
You asked me what I wanted then,
I said, "nothing"
But kisses sinned...

Something about the way
We touched,
The powerful way
Your soul made thrust,
Before the clothes embraced floors trust—
You removed the layer of fear that stood between us...

We never finished,
what began—
*Life and choices became our **Friends**,*
Sometimes,
I wonder if we'd be two
To be continued- indeed rings true...

FINGERPAINT

Play with me—
Know when gently
Know when rough
Like you found artisanship worthy to **Etch**
Your wood
Tie me right
Bend my yes into strings singing—
Tongues that even God would blush with the understanding.

With one hand entangled in the hair of my
Mind
And the other
Slid between the thighs of self-will
Until the only thing my pen can do is
Fucklust
With an intensity
That caused drips of surrender
To splatter
Like thoughts caught in between
My soul's page creases—
You stained my moans into signatures...

NOVICE

My arousal was coming of age
Finally understanding the curves of my will
The slopes of my hesitations
The peaks and valleys of reckless cascades
Like nature, it sang out to the sun to be touched
And like the wild, it howled at the moon to be set free
*Our touch become **Roots**,*
how they danced naked on the soil of his tongue
trees of my surrender springing up as living waters—
He drank into dehydration…

ASPHYXIA

Drown me in temptations
Leave my life aching in healed
*Swell my lungs with inhales of **Adored***
Leave my hesitations limp and lifeless
With the touch of your sacrifice
Bruise my soul's lips with your love

FOREPLAY

Go deeper
With each thrust of acceptance
I find myself lying across your mind's counter top—
soul completely naked

Parted thighs of clarity form guiding glasses to see quakes of
vulnerability
Pages of skin becoming tracing paper for the pen of your tongue as
you stain your name
You keep me coming—
arching towards your safe
trembling towards your love
uttering incoherently towards
your compassion
You pull me…
His pull-out game was strong

SEQUENCE

Eyes that hit the room in my soul marked slowly,
Your essence walked over to me—tapping my senses on the shoulder.
Without a word,
your presence took my willpower's hand, and then slowly,
My heartbeat followed your pace down the hall of vulnerability.
*We passed the art on the wall marked **Apprehensions**,*
Approaching the door to surrender,
your patience stopped at the knob—
The seduction in your hesitation whispered deeply—
*on, in, with, **YOU**, can I be...*

CHANNEL

You bent me over and broke my sweat like perfume,
the scent of your surrender
dripped down my soul—
my freedom never smelled better...

MANTRA

I wanna fall into the depth of undone with you
take the risk of unadulterated bliss
drip with the taste of your pain's surrender
shiver from the touch of your complete acceptance
while arching to the melody of your vulnerability singing trust.

and then,

Seduce the innocence of your hidden shadows
satiate the thirst of your honor
pulsate from the thrust of your reserve
pant into delirium while kissing your smile
slip into speech impediments from the whisper of your soul.

and then,

Etch my name into your legacy—
so even your ancestors' pain can't wait to wear it.
So many things will fall again
for now,
let my aches as they scribble,
fall tenderly into a thought—

SMEAR

Maybe just maybe,
I like the thought of your pages creasing—
Ink swelling into cursive imprints…
Lips tracing your yes, into lines wet from soaking the soul

Maybe just maybe,
I like hands typing your curiosity into pants—
spine binds of choice pressed into
Flat arching…
The will of my thighs lying open

Maybe just maybe,
I like your pen tasting my talent—
Drippings onto pages of your succumbing…
Plain sheets awaiting the spillage of your soul in color

Your chapters look powerful—
let's see you defile my ink…

WHISKEY

Stare at me,
long, then hard—
I'm a sip that masters any bottle
with a whisper, you can pour.

Take me into your inhale,
like a rim, let it rest on your lips—
Swirl the motions of my ease,
turn this ink into my hips

Like that smile that is emerging,
taste of sweetness which can't be
bought—
Spill me just a little,
onto the clothing of your thoughts...

FIRST

We were young
Breathless
Inexperienced in this backseat of life
Clawing at the clothes of movie scenes
Imitating the movements of cyclones
We were young
Exhausted
Minutes that masked as hours
As we wondered what next,
making eye contact with avoidance…

SOILED

Close your eyes
Bide your time
Think on list
Avoid the kiss
Pay your dues
Soul need not exist
Let him buck
Paying for safety—
receipt marked—violence's' dry fuck…

NEAT

My hairdo is flawless
Every pin in place
Not a strand out of its moment
No sweat dripping in face
A picture of perfection
On this wedding day
No curl missing a step
Even after we lay
So I pick up the phone
And a bobby pin falls
Knowing he will make a war zone appear on the nape of this neck
After I hang up this call…

MOONLIGHTING

I work the red light district
Lipstick words on whiskey-stained loneliness
High heels of a moment
Walking across the floor of sorrow
Hiked-up skirt of responsibilities
Expose lie's inward thighs
As I succumb to, desire for hire
Me his wife, praying for death or to one day be fired

SCRIBBLES

I could hear nature singing
as you kissed me deep
Or maybe
it was my bones becoming music notes against the softness
Of your skin
You took your time with each moment
An endless pen, writing a novel to my orgasms
And when you finished,
I was a notebook
Inscribed like the signature of your smell...

PARCHED

You taste like a mistake
I thirst to know—
Just how human it is to, error...

DAYDREAMS

Fantasy island is where we lived
You would call me when she left your bed
And I would text you when he fell deep asleep
We would rip panties where the ocean breathed
I could raise a mountain under the canvas of those pants
And you could drown continents when I heard a gesture of your hand
So the moments grew and grew
No harm, nor foul, and forever no meet—
Just **Fantasy Island** of imaginations that creep

SALUTED

Standing at the shorelines
Tear stains left my eyes intoxicated
His touch was startling, a stranger asking if I'm okay
Making rounds to keep the neighborhood safe
So cute how he wondered how to make sure I was comforted
And his tone changed as I walked, his shadow suggesting— stay a bit
It was arousing how he looked at me, standing tall in the moonlight
Thank you, for the stars you gave that night
Against the ocean's midnight canvas
This smile got home safely
Making love on the hood of a squad car—
Protected, Served, a Patriot indeed—that day

130

SIGNAL

Raindrops fall—
Hard then soft
Rapidly, then drizzled—
Clouds pant in exuberance
And in exhaustion…

Like telekinesis,
I hear the whispers of the downpour,
arching and rolling into surrendered puddles—
licking restraint as they slide down the car—
I match torrential storm within,
relentlessly,
feverishly,
and, without shelter—
my fingers moan your name
*into **Morse** code…*

OXYGEN

Your touch told me
I was suffocating,
So I breathed you in
like a patient in need of respiratory therapy—
One. Suck. At. A. Time.

ADDICTION

He wanted me
Like a kid wanted candy in a store falling out on the floor
Like the sunlight wanted to caress the petals of a flower into bloom
Like the moon wanted the dark to pull the hair of its stars
and ride it into the glistening we bask in
He wanted…

AFTERBURN

Straddling you in this chair
Hair falling to my waist
Hands cupping my ass
Treasure maps finding x across your face
I love to take you in, slow
And work just the tip
I can feel your legs trembling
While you bit your lips
I'm swollen from entry—you are rather big
but you are my favorite toy and I am a Toys-R-Us kid
Don't mess it up,
you just did—damn, now there went the thrill
When will you all learn
saying, "I love you," kills…

PORTRAIT

trepidation like a gown has slipped off my being—
Lying here immersed between the sheets of insanity and enthrallment,
The pearls of evidence,
Gathering like silken drops reviving my soul…
That whisper, umm…
How it's the
sweetness that colors my mind into shades of
Lace…
Now do what you know best,
slide my self-control to the side,
and finger paint a masterpiece...

PEELED

Skin to soul
Heart to hand
Caresses to tongued passion, panting in semantics—
One tug of your realness
And the strings of my fears unravel before you
Hot. Moist. Spread.

INTOXICATED

I tasted your mind before I tasted your lips—some kiss as foreplay,
I kiss like a fuck—
intensely, deadly—
with every intention of making you,
tongue-tied with my name...
Having never savored the touch of addiction before,
I bit my lower lip and fingered an even lower one,
I had you sliding down the seat,
creating puddles of surrender in the car...God,
how I needed that passion,
that overwhelming yearning to simply just be—uncontrollably wanted
Parked Confessions—watching the couple in the next car

SIPS

Slide down my throat like the sweetest of sugar cane
I got a Taste for gluttony
feed me more of your salutations at attention
These lips need licking
You can get to my lower later
Nothing is sweeter than that uncontrolled clench of hair...

BECKON

Songbird
come be my after party
dim the lights on misery
turn up the bubble bath
of found so keep
come lick between thighs until
my skin screams free

136

CORNUCOPIAS

My soul,
A drought—
Famished and Desolate...

You,
torrential downpours—
Nourishment seeping into
the very cracks of my essence...

Like Fire seducing ice,
My heart's soul is saturated—
flip me like tillage
And harvest my possibilities...

DRENCHED

In the thundering rain,
tasting the night breeze
turning this mind to handcuffs
let me be your body's party

OWN

Rip my soul wide open
Spilling the wetness of my patience
Tongue my essence
Until my fantasies are left longing
Arch my vulnerability
Parting my hesitations upon glistening lips
My temptations panting and waiting—
Fuck holding back,
Pull the hair of my life and make it say your name...

GLISTEN

I long to be the sheet your soul wraps in...
Soiled by the pleasure of your thoughts
Crumpled from the wrestling of your whisper
Dampened by the sweat of trust...

RUB

As candlelight serenades the moon,
and the skin plays host, hope breathes
Like thoughts that moan of desire louder than midnight winds
shivers become instruments playing for the tongue
As sweats of faith dampen each moment
and transparency plays charades between intertwined bodies
sheets of **Misgivings** crumple on repeat—
canvases of passions, smudging hearts, like a thumbprint...

ACROSTIC

Fingered hauntingly, my arch compelled.
Unnerving my mantra of pants, savagely.
Caught, the scent of your revive within this orgasm.
Kismet, the taste you leave within pulsating lips, opened.
Linger.
Usurp this need for my arch to keep control.
Send sensations through divided thighs like a cunt seeking a
        sanctuary of semen.
Taste every drop of your name being spelled, rapidly.

CHURCH

Like a confessional, place me upon your lips,
let the taste of my arch
open the mouth of your mind until—
your moan welcomes damnation in such a way,
that even Hail Mary, becomes a Hell of a Merry, panting in bliss.
If I let the straddle of my yes,
And
the slip of my resist fall around your ankles,
will you drop to bended knee to drink the wine of my time
or
will your worship leave you tongue-tied in thighed rhymes

Like stained glass riding the tongue of sunlight,
 christen my body with the holy grail of your touch,
until the drips of sweat are deemed anointing oil
         that even hell begs to be doused of...

SIGNALS

*I struggled with the thoughts of how you play-**OUT**—*
in this ink, that is.
And I've wrestled with images of dampened sheets—
*Found myself panting, like letters written by **Keats**.*
Somehow, I've kept at bay,
*the traces of your lip-**PRINTS**—on the mirrors of my want.*
Now, I sit folded like creases of pages,
where I succumb to your taunts.

Lay me now, like a bookmark of trust,
and bend this will,
until smudged pages lie in stained thrust.
Say what you want and don't hold back.

Teach Morse, my code—
show Braille what it lacks.
The quill is in your hands,
my book spread—on the floor—
Come into my chapters slowly—
fill each line you adore.

Position this footnote,
don't lose count of each—
Initialed, an author in waiting,
*of your press—**RELEASE**...*

FORGED ♦ IN ♦ INK

Here you read the lace of my mind. Moments that have been and some to come. The shedding of clothes by ink. Sometimes it was of free will, often not, but the lessons learned, my pages have taught.

I've learned to harness and bridle the tempest of nude, but that doesn't mean I can wear inked lingerie before you...
*I like being **Naked**, how about you...*

<u>S K I N</u>

Wear your heart on your skin in this lfe.

Sylvia Plath

FORGED ♦ IN ♦ INK

See you, I do—
parts of hope,
scraps of pleads—
a sarcophagus of love
trying to find your living trust amongst the dead.
Hear you, I am—
melody of cautions
lyrics of needs—
a symphony of abundance
longing to play the crescendo of safe for an audience of one.
Feel you, I can—
vulnerability of soul, caresses of open- a stripping of whispers,
bellowing into the yes of touched—
goosebumps tracing acceptance,
*into—**SKIN**...*

A voice I have longed to hear—
destiny, eavesdropping on the soul,
as light glanced at dark—
       Their smile combusted
         into color.

A whisper I have waited to learn—
familiar, pulling my curiosity into waves.
as oceans serenade shores—
       Swirls of serendipity
       create braille for hope.

A presence I have surrendered to enjoy—
stillness, purpose bending the curves of me—
as gentle moves silently into heightened moments
       Shadows of each reflection of me remain locked in
       *forehead kisses—**Reality***

I became a sip to remember
And
My self-esteem
*Became an alcoholic—**Sober***

FORGED ◆ IN ◆ INK

I shed some old mindsets
forged my pieces into wallpaper
I think this house is coming together nicely
living, feeling, crying, sighing, middle fingers, and silence
*painting the walls of—**ME***

Let me be the healing balm to the scars of your life
let me be the restoration to your fountain of youth
I will be gentle
*Now, take my hand, whispered—**Choices***

*These **Scars** are **Beauty Marks** that show*
how people have been torn
and
*put back together with—**flare***

FORGED ◆ IN ◆ INK

(For my fellow Cancer Survivors)

You would have me think that my femininity was defiled
You would have me believe that my woman
was confiscated
You would have me plead that my essence
was diluted You would have me state that my value
was depleted

You would have me dissect the life of me
just to settle for fear and disbelief
You would have me discount the value that I still share
and refuse to accept that my wholeness is alive if I dare

I am more than the scars of your knife
I am greater than the outcome of this plight
I am a marker of resilience over fear
The mantra that a fighter in me is still reigning near
I am still woman, hear me roar
I am still vibrant even with differences gracing my shores
I am still phenomenal and worthy of this smile

You had left me in ashes, but my beauty resounds
So now I will take the remnants of what was left
and create a charcoal masterpiece with overcoming's imprint

You said many things, but I'm no caged bird
I have beaten your sayings and changed your words—

I AM STILL HERE

*Defying odds once again—**PHOENIX***

I could tell you of the endless thoughts that I count of you—
but I've never seen the grains of sand numbered
I could sing of the smile you leave across my lips—
but I've yet to find words with enough rhythm to match your essence
I could drink in your presence like a desert finding oasis—
*but I've nothing left unquenched amid a **Tsunami***
I could inscribe the way your ambiance creates an impression—
but that would be like harnessing the sun into a pen…
*I could say so much, but who can truly label—**PEACE***

Collateral damage for charges other blew
The shrapnel of their disloyalty and antics
Speaking like a severed aorta— distrust
Actions speak louder than words
But only when one has something they know to prove,
*not unknown—yet needed—**Closure**.*

What if I lay my mind on the line
And strip the clothing of my apprehension
Slowly—
Undressing the timidity of acceptance,
Unbuttoning the security of familiarity,
The garments of self-consciousness
Slipping off—
Until standing before your soul is nothing more than...
*the lace of reciprocity—**Boundaries***

If you let me walk the corridors of your time,
I promise that I will bring enough light for a one-way trip.
I have no desire to find my way out,
I only know that your heartbeat is the map,
*guiding my soul's compass—**Arriving***

FORGED ♦ IN ♦ INK

Revive my appetite,
cause my circumspection to fall like drops of water,
poignantly soaking
dehydrated lips;
like a chair firmly planted,
be the taste where my soul can rest.

Cradle my hesitancy,
like shallow breaths learning their pulse, become rhythm creating
exhales through consistency—
trust contracting to finally find muscle relaxation.

Deserted in journey,
a heart mummified with beauty untapped,
a relic being sought without being found—
so much love bound in burial graves—
*travesty's treasure, offering map—**Exhaling***

FORGED ◆ IN ◆ INK

Trepidation, like a gown
slips off my being—
My courage, lying immersed between
sheets of insanity and enthrallment

These pearls, surrender's evidence,
gathering like silken drops—
Revived, my soul whispers,
as security colors my mind

Like wings finally found,
my smile's span, you open—How exquisite—
that when I look to the skies jealous that they see you endlessly,
they too, look back at you with admiration,
whispering how they can compete with such,
*Defining Horizons—***Free Will***

SCHOOL DAZE

Like a child discovering the sunlight,
Or the first time, a breeze hits the skin—
Stand in the rain of my smile.

Come play in the sands of my patience—
Lose yourself in the library of my trust
Come, let your needs
run away with me—
*I am a recess full of peace—***Reconciliation***...*

Many can slide on
Facade with a whisper—
But none can wear
this essence- it's not store-bought— ***Authenticity***

FORGED ♦ IN ♦ INK

Like piano keys
listening to the lyrics of anticipation,
I find myself held captive by the sound of pause—

Pause of fears
Pause of longings
Pause of doubts
Pause of empty

Sitting here,
listening to the ink spill out diaries—
surrender becomes drenched pages of
eyes witnessing—

Friendship forming into fingerprints
Understood serenading as smudges
Consistency outlining into calligraphy

Like piano keys
I found myself, listening—
as sheet music between readiness of soul
*and finality of solidification—**Smile**...*

Across the galaxy of this mind,
I watched you like a shooting star—
picking up the stardust from where your last wish had fallen.

Within the botanical of the soul,
I caught wind of your essence—
the aroma of hope still lying like dew
Permeating petals of "what if..."

Falling into the familiarity of my own smile,
Like hands caressing the curve of a guitar—
surrendering has become
The sweetest lyric
As I play self-confidence
*like melodies envied by heaven—**Comfortable***

In the moment of a thought,
The cup of reasoning poured.
Careless whispers sang the night to the wind,
As my hope laid unfolded,
*The shape of resilience in heart—**Origami***

My soul's taste buds are drawn to the sweetness of your wild—
the aroma of your confidence,
like nectar—permeates as whispers,
dripping down my resistance.

Cradle this vulnerability—
ripen my concession,
leave bite marks of longing—
hunger lacerating whatever was left of my hesitation.
I am ready to become yours
And you enter me as mine,

Like skin,
*consider my caution peeled—***Passion Fruit***

FORGED ♦ IN ♦ INK

So fragile, a moment in time...
As the grains of sand fall by the hour
so do the roots of my fear.
Like the snowflake hiking on the passions of the sun,
succumb to the breaking away of familiar and free-fall
carelessly, unimpeded as it learns the surrender in melt,
I too am finding freedom in the slow drip of hesitation undoing—**Life**

I am not weakness
I am humility with a heartbeat
I am the oasis of hope springing up in a drought of cast aside
I am glory falling into the inhale of
Shadows becoming light
It is not weakness to see another and extend hands to brush off the
dirt and abuse of ignored
It takes great strength to love like skin—
elastic, covering, fragile, yet layered...
I am not weakness
I am destiny clothed in purpose
You don't just wear the skin of my essence
You adorn—**Coronations**

To be a genie in a bottle
The ghost on the wind
A shooting promise leaving stardust
Like an ocean's breeze, take me in.

Looked at without touch
Felt, void of understood
Reviving as moments cause drowning
Causing the sun's heartbeat, to desire crowing.

Creating taste buds for the soul
Giving voice to your dreams
Come rub my mind's fabric
Seamless pleats labeled a heart maverick—**Garments**

Skin and attention
climb the same striptease pole
While depth and decency
become a silent black and white film—
a theater on the verge of shut down—**Praise**

Not one to give voice up easily
takes a moment to hear the whisper roar
but when the heart is full, not empty—
cards that fall reflect what is sure

Some deal the game of wanderings
as the sands of time fall through these hands
many players manhandled this shuffle—
yet, I'm a gamble worth the command

Anything but a simple spade to behold
this smile that roulette has dealt
so much calm lies before you
like a hurricane—
*restrained in **Silk**...*

I get pain, and I understand the hurt,
but I can't make a mausoleum out of agony.
Everything in life is felt,
but what a person does only has so much impact
before it starts becoming
what YOU keep redoing to YOU.
It takes courage, breaking the cycle,
*and building something new—**Hypothesizing***

FORGED ♦ IN ♦ INK

I just wanna write pretty words
Or stain tears through ink
Drop heart into lines
And sign my name like a paper cut

I just wanna like the boy
Or doodle my thoughts in smiles
Get back to my basic
And love simplicity like a fresh-cut flower

I just wanna crease my being in humility
Or spill out like a bookmark indent
Draft moments into timestamps
And leave the spotlight on for the next pen…

*I just wanna—**Soul Exhale***

I can let go instantly,
But not without carvings to the wall of my soul
Where hope last scratched for chance's breath
And the veins of my courage collapse in need of supply
But should I find a smile worth the beat
That drives my heart
And my pulse for yearning regains consciousness
Like a Phoenix discovering feathers of fire
I will burn with an intensity that reduces even the sun
*into steam—**Rhythm***

Let me be the sun that heats your pulse
the moon that lights your heartbeat
the stars of that hurt smile
when the world seems to spin without the light of your ways
I will be there to hold you down
if you need a heart that can beat under siege
if you need a smile that can see you without pleads
if you need a touch that can feel you without the threat of skin
*Let me, Self-Worth—**Diamond***

Stumbled across tears gathering storm clouds to roar...
Sunlight leaves smudge marks of inspiration across my faceL
ike a whirlwind coming to an end,
labored lungs begin to inhale—
I'm not a butterfly to catch in a net
Not some trophy to be had for the sake of fascination
But, see me,
a Monarch,
just as I am.
I am better than catch and release
My wings, chest pounds crying out in exhales—
*You wear winged crowns—know your identity—**Wings***

If the ache of love
must take place
Then I'm making each racing pulse
*my bitch—**Dominatrix***

FORGED ♦ IN ♦ INK

Here I am in fragrance and myth
humble beginnings, a muck
the offering of myself
the aroma of my bliss

Here I am in fragility of oil
singing in cascades to the feet of peace
the broken counterparts of story untold
ready to be spread as an aroma of gold

Here I am in this alabaster box
the good and the bad summed up in cost
the spillage of sacrifices called the reflection of me
*now laying open, poured out to be seen—***Emerging**

If I must wear
the touch of encountering you—
it will be as a beauty mark
*clawing from its scar—***Warrior**

FORGED ♦ IN ♦ INK

I'm not going to apologize for being who or how I am!
I know what low-crawl it took
I know what mire muck I had to wade through
The fears & tears that struck the sight of my worth

I'm not going to apologize for being who or how I am!
I know the shadows from forsaken abyss I rose from
I know the ashes to masterpiece my blood mixed
The abandonment and rejections of lies that kiss
I'm not going to apologize for the scars I chiseled into beauty marks
I know the shrapnel pieces that I had to call armor
I know the jagged glass edges that created the thorns seen as petals
The constant perspiration my hope sweats
*as it walks the hallways of "hell" called life—**Optimistic***

There is a speech that leaves whispers deemed loud.
A silence that screams deaf into concert.
A realization that leaves the mind illiterate—
much like the rain that drops in a single serenade,
or the shores
who stripe in vulnerability within a kiss from the ocean...

There is a You,
that wrecks this bunkered shelter,
*called me into Architecture—**Edifices***

FORGED ♦ IN ♦ INK

I'm not going to apologize
Instead, I will rise
Smell my aroma or walk on by

I'm not going to hide that I no longer despise
The moments that cards dealt removed all disguise

I am what I am

Beauty, but make no mistake, I too am beast—
I can break a soul in an instance,
just as much as bring peace

I'm not going to apologize
So, if you come my way
I am the crown of resiliency's jewel

You are welcomed at my table
or stay at bay

I'm damaged goods, turned gourmet fuel
You can starve or feast
the entree is up to you
But what I never serve up is being a fool

*I'm not going to apologize—**Reign***

FORGED ♦ IN ♦ INK

She spoke in cuddles and cheek strokes of tears, being wiped.
Mother inspiration, pouring her heartbeat and cloaking breastplate
upon abandonment's nursery.

Growing pulses into arrayed flowers—blooms that forever became
essence, only floating like aroma.

But when the sunlight laid down at night,
her moonlight watered in tears, roses in concrete
with bloodstained thorns—
*Crowns being... **Birthed***

You were a gentle beauty,
like ink breathing calligraphy
A moment of heartbeat,
like fingerpaint and a child

The sound of desire announcing birth,
like thunder bowing to lightning—
Time batted eyes,
and for a split second of oneness,
the Earth stood still in wonder of elements called—
*your essence—**Reflections***

FORGED ♦ IN ♦ INK

A dream, simplest of fantasy,
knock upon the mystery that I call door—
allow curiosity to bridge anxiety and peace—
crashed waves—you the hunger,
        my gentle the shores...

Such a sun, who lacks knowledge,
soaking clouds with the worth of its shine—
an axis, created to orbit the planets—
a diamond rolling around like a marble
          as if common is your kind...

My soul sees you, maybe because I too, hide,
the shadows of ashes I have lived—
masterpieces of charcoal, pilot-less—
as I rest in the background
        like the color of blend...

Within the silence, ink spills like braille,
carrying whispers the winds hold—
like loose leaf edges, you are paper soaked into plight—
hurt carved into the soul
        like works of living art...

With all the frames that surround you,
and sears of etchings that leave scars if even for a moment,
*you remember this kiss has called them—**Beauty***

FORGED ◆ IN ◆ INK

I am Reserved,
not Timid.
I am Restored,
not Tarnished.
I am Revived,
not Trampled.

I am Reborn,
not Tragic.

I am, simply exhausted manifestation—
strength learning plea,
exhale singing caged,
hope lit with wet matches...

I am,
*just, real roaring in whispers—**Self***

Never was the type to play with the clothing of
my time,
presence
or heart,
But my essence when someone is real—
*consider me unzipped showing—**SKIN**...*

"What are you made for?" said, my eyes to—
paper,
heart to the ink,
sound to the silence within the tears that scream.

"What are you made of?" said, thoughts—
shallow in breathing,
rapid in courage swallowing,
terror in this grounded spirit, made for heights—yet waddling.

"What are you...?" said, this pause before truth—
let down's in reflection,
tenacity covered sweat finding direction,
finality's letter of acceptance—an entrance to embrace imperfections.

Just inked hot pursuits,
*Wanting the reclaiming of my "You", Honestly—***Transpicuous***

"What are you wearing,"
My fears asked my courage.
"Distinguished, and I'm fucking dripping in it...' said, ***Maturity***

FORGED ♦ IN ♦ INK

Sometimes,
You just have to accept- you're
tender-hearted
that hopeless romantic
that bubbly optimistic

Sometimes,
You just have to accept- you're
an ocean's wave without a shore
a sunrise set in a black hole
the serenity of nature with no scenery given

Sometimes,
You just have to accept- you're
tears that can't accumulate for the shed
fears too paralyzed for a soul to acknowledge
Quiet that does nothing but scream

Sometimes, just sometimes,
You have to accept being human—
imperfection's balance
of learn & live—

And yet, sometimes,
in that moment
when you're ready to be ready no more,
steady your shakes

*Because sometimes, resurrection will only come through—***Press***

FORGED ♦ IN ♦ INK

The only time I understand me
Is In the closet of pages of thee
Line by line I find my way
Turning each corner inviting smile to stay
Wonders never cease
Pain has a cure
Romance lives brighter
Creases being assured
I can reach out deeply with all might
Into the inventions of imagination's sight
Torrential downpours of inked voices bleed
Line by line my soul does read
And so, I curl up once again
And climb these literary staircases
Without end
And here I sit nestled with glee
*waiting for how new ink will transport me—**Teleported***

I see the brightest horizons upon the lips of the mind.
Spread like eternity and damnation—
a gasp and inhale all within a moment—
the smile that says come closer.

I hear the songs of peace like a nest beckoning a bird—
the sweetest chirps of lost and found; a treasure map and fools gold,
intertwined as passive glances that whisper—like sunlight screams.

I...
at least that is what touch-sentenced to fire,
told soothe-sipping imagination's water of hope—
*seduction through soul inhalations...**Book of Breathing***

Undress my fears
Slide the skirt of my apprehension to the floor
Lead me to the bed of your understanding
Lie me down onto the pillow of your safety
Partnership, not just because of intimacy,
But because our love language speaks
In-to-me-see

Rest for me—
Like a stream, fluid in cracking rocks,
Allow your fear's mind to find solitude near the currents of my
embrace
Like a soft breeze bringing relief,
My trust will be an oasis on the dry, cracked, skin of your heart
Lie back in the grass of healing's essence—
My lap is a meadow of splendor for the insomnia of acceptance
Rest for me—
As the sway of admiration rocks you to sleep through lullabies of
acceptance
Breathe it in,
This aroma of sincerity, as the vulnerabilities of my rosebuds,
perfume your soul
And just like that,
Transparency becomes a pillow for the soul and heart to talk…
Mates

And if I asked you—
"How do you see you?"
Would your heart fight for the glasses or your fears—
*Shivers in moments, standing before my—**Identity.***

Battles within caused questions to arise.
But it wasn't until my shadows saw the beauty of sunlight
nd my moments found shelter in the dark,
That I understood
Stepping into purpose means stepping out of familiarity and comfort
You already know how to stay,
*Leave footprints on the back of destiny's neck—***Statements***

Sometimes in life,
One must lay in the sands of chance—
Letting the waves of opportunity carry you,
not to safety,
*but... to experience—***Mastery***...*

Falling into your arms is the most unintentional bliss…
Lying here, the intensity of your presence consumes
You embrace me in my rise
You kiss me in my slumber
This is a romance no fairy-tale's articulation could convey
You draw me & flee me all at once—
*Time, you are a bittersweet—**Enchantment***

Illumination that pierces the deepest darkness…
Radiance that subdues willpower into complete surrender…
Vibrancy that colors the heart into perfection's canvas…
What is this experience consuming the soul's essence—
*You leave such inviting lipstick prints from your smile—**Hope***

What will it take to awaken the eyes of the soul
Will it take the kiss of inspiration
The discipline of dedication
Gentle whispers of the heart's aspirations
What will it take to awaken the eyes of the soul
Many dreams lie destitute incapacitated with wonder...
*Pick up your—***Driven**

People who only want to fit in,
will capitalize off of standing on you
to be better viewed—
Loyal as a leaf in the wind...
People who naturally fit in,
well, they will know that truth,
but, they love with their authenticity,
like a branch gives legacy to a leaf,
*they give shoulder—***Stand & Deliver**

You are like the perfect stranger;
the sound of your voice has peaked my curiosities sentiments...
The smell of your presence has incited an allure...
Glancing at your smile is to behold the ensnarement of addiction...
With just one gesture...
I am rendered defenseless—
compelled—
constrained—
I follow...
Without hesitation—
remorse—
encumbrance—
against a wall I find you...
Precision of your touch has slid my rationale slowly to the side...
Inability to resist, our eyes hold each other....
Standing before you—
my predilection aroused to transparency...
At this moment all that matters is the sound you cause me to make...
Is it wrong for me to want another chance encounter...
Open me—
*aspirations need a rendezvous today—**Endless Potential**...*

FORGED ♦ IN ♦ INK

So broken, said the soul to the mind
Said the body to the will
Said the life to the smile…

So broken, said the dreams to the whisper
Said the courage to the vision
Said the strength to the struggle…

And yet…
You
Are
Still
Here…

Said the spirit to the heartbeat
Said the pulse to the rise
Said the voice to the exhale…

You
Can't
Stay
Broken…

Said the hopes to the potential
Said the hearing to the silence
Said the chance to the unknown…
Now, what will you do…
*Said I to ME…holding the mirror…called—**YOU***

I'd lie in your hand like a pen,
Just to feel your essence curse
My ink.

I'd stretch out like a line,
Just to feel the press of thoughts
inscribed.

I'd live as the brim of your mind,
Just to title the legacy of your
transparency.

I'd do so many things
With your blank—
Signed,
*waiting for its name—**Existence***

FORGED ♦ IN ♦ INK

You will not make my soul bleed again
I am not the scars you left on my heart
I am risen ashes
breath from trauma's suffocation
purpose from violated promise
resilience rebelling against demolition
I AM *hope etched—**Alive***

I asked my reflection a question—
my soul answered instead

Surrounded by an audience of
Crumpled pleas—
each a masterpiece,

Endorsed by the same poet—
*Liquid vulnerability—**Afterbirth***

FORGED ♦ IN ♦ INK

There is a beauty that creates earthquakes—
confidence that scorches so intensely,
the sun is mistaken for a burnt-out match
Still,
I could create an entire galaxy
with the depth of just your glance and yet,
the solar system couldn't spin your charisma day or night

If what has passed is a total eclipse,
then you have become the gravitational pull of my smile's heartbeat

so kill me softly
As I do believe in second breaths,
the melody of rising, humming softly,
still distant in soul—
perhaps, a song, that one day,
my surrender will sing,
and stars will name each other after our glimmer—
*a cosmos of Self-Acceptance—**Galaxies***

No, she isn't the softest girl,
Life has put her soul at war—
Shards of glass,
Shaped like resilience
Thorns of grit,
Covering the stem of her identity
Petals of iron,
masking hemorrhaging that flow
Passion and perspective,
perfumed from broken bottles
dripping tenacity
No, she isn't the softest girl,
She is deliberate—

*She, is woman—**QUEEN***

FORGED ♦ IN ♦ INK

Many are the pages our choices write.
One day, they will be the novel in which,
the heart's survival must choose to read...

—Avant Avant-garde

ABOUT THE AUTHOR

Avant Avant-garde is a profuse lover of words. They are her saving grace and the hellfire of how she draws breath. She was inspired at an early age by the classic poets who have paved the way for modern day poetry.

As she puts it, poetry is the calligraphy of the soul.

Avant is a voice for all writers and artists. Her personal writer's page, and several others she writes for are dedicated to being an advocate for writers of all levels, across various social media platforms and published works.

Follow her writing at facebook.com/SavantAvantGarde

FORGED ♦ IN ♦ INK